I0455864

April 2016

K-12 EDUCATION

Better Use of Information Could Help Agencies Identify Disparities and Address Racial Discrimination

GAO-16-345

K-12 EDUCATION

Better Use of Information Could Help Agencies Identify Disparities and Address Racial Discrimination

Highlights of GAO-16-345, a report to congressional requesters

Why GAO Did This Study

Recent literature shows that poor and minority students may not have full access to educational opportunities. GAO was asked to examine poverty and race in schools and efforts by the Departments of Education and Justice, which are responsible for enforcing federal civil rights laws prohibiting racial discrimination against students.

This report examined (1) how the percentage of schools with high percentages of poor and Black or Hispanic students has changed over time and the characteristics of these schools, (2) why and how selected school districts have implemented actions to increase student diversity, and (3) the extent to which the Departments of Education and Justice have taken actions to identify and address issues related to racial discrimination in schools.

GAO analyzed Education data for school years 2000-01 to 2013-14 (most recent available); reviewed applicable federal laws, regulations, and agency documents; and interviewed federal officials, civil rights and academic subject matter specialists, and school district officials in three states, selected to provide geographic diversity and examples of actions to diversify.

What GAO Recommends

GAO recommends that Education more routinely analyze its civil rights data to identify disparities among types and groups of schools and that Justice systematically track key information on open federal school desegregation cases to which it is a party to better inform its monitoring. In response, both agencies are considering actions in line with GAO's recommendations.

View GAO-16-345. For more information, contact Jacqueline M. Nowicki (617) 788-0580 or nowickij@gao.gov.

What GAO Found

The percentage of K-12 public schools in the United States with students who are poor and are mostly Black or Hispanic is growing and these schools share a number of challenging characteristics. From school years 2000-01 to 2013-14 (the most recent data available), the percentage of all K-12 public schools that had high percentages of poor and Black or Hispanic students grew from 9 to 16 percent, according to GAO's analysis of data from the Department of Education (Education). These schools were the most racially and economically concentrated: 75 to 100 percent of the students were Black or Hispanic and eligible for free or reduced-price lunch—a commonly used indicator of poverty. GAO's analysis of Education data also found that compared with other schools, these schools offered disproportionately fewer math, science, and college preparatory courses and had disproportionately higher rates of students who were held back in 9th grade, suspended, or expelled.

In the three districts GAO reviewed as case studies, officials reported implementing various actions to increase economic and racial diversity to address racial or other demographic shifts in school composition. For example, in one predominantly low-income, Black and Hispanic school district, the state and district created state-of-the-art magnet schools to attract students from more economically and racially diverse groups. However, these three districts faced challenges. For example, one state devoted funding to magnet schools while the district's traditional schools declined in quality, according to local officials. Further, according to officials, some magnets with openings could not accept minority students because doing so would interfere with the ratio of minority to non-minority students that the district was trying to achieve.

The Departments of Education and Justice have taken a range of actions to identify and address racial discrimination against students. Education has investigated schools, analyzed its data by student groups protected under federal civil rights laws, and found discrimination and disparities in some cases. GAO analyzed Education's data among types of schools (charters, magnets, and traditional public schools) by percentage of racial minorities and a proxy for poverty level and found multiple disparities, including in access to academic courses. Education does not routinely analyze its data in this way. Conducting this type of analysis would enhance Education's ability to target technical assistance and identify other disparities by school types and groups. The Department of Justice (Justice) has also investigated discrimination claims, and it monitors and enforces 178 open federal desegregation court cases to which it is a party, many of which originated 30 or 40 years ago to remedy segregation. However, GAO found that Justice does not track key summary case information, such as the last action taken in a case. As a result, some may unintentionally remain dormant for long periods. For example, in one case the court noted there had been a lack of activity and that if Justice had "been keeping an eye" on relevant information, such as test score disparities, the issue could have been addressed in a more timely way. Federal internal control standards state that agencies should use information to help identify specific actions that need to be taken to allow for effective monitoring. Without tracking key information about open cases, Justice's ability toward effectively monitor such cases is hampered.

_____ United States Government Accountability Office

Contents

Tables

Figures

Abbreviations

AP	Advanced Placement
CCD	Common Core of Data
Civil Rights Data	Civil Rights Data Collection
Education	U.S. Department of Education
EL	English Learners
GATE	Gifted and Talented Education
H/PBH	High-Poverty and mostly Black or Hispanic
IB	International Baccalaureate
Justice	U.S. Department of Justice
K-12	Kindergarten through 12th grade
L/PBH	Low-Poverty and fewer Black or Hispanic
STEM	Science, Technology, Engineering, and Mathematics

441 G St. N.W.
Washington, DC 20548

April 21, 2016

The Honorable John Conyers, Jr.
Ranking Member
Committee on the Judiciary
House of Representatives

The Honorable Robert C. "Bobby" Scott
Ranking Member
Committee on Education and the Workforce
House of Representatives

After the landmark 1954 ruling by the United States Supreme Court in *Brown v. Board of Education of Topeka,* which found racial segregation in public schools to violate the U.S. Constitution, many schools were required to take action to desegregate.[1] Subsequent federal legislation, including the Civil Rights Act of 1964, was enacted to prohibit racial discrimination in public schools; the workplace; and in places that serve the public, such as hotels, restaurants, and theaters. While much has changed in public education in the decades following this landmark decision and subsequent legislative action, research has shown that some of the most vexing issues affecting children and their access to educational excellence and opportunity today are inextricably linked to race and poverty. At the backdrop of these issues, a history of discriminatory practices has contributed to inequities in education for some students. Further, efforts to increase the diversity of schools are hampered sometimes because the composition of neighborhood schools is often a microcosm of children's neighborhoods. Thus, children who live in neighborhoods with a high minority population and with high levels of poverty tend to go to schools mirroring these demographics.

---

[1] In *Brown,* which consolidated four separate cases from different states, the U.S. Supreme Court held that the intentional segregation of children on the basis of race in public schools violates the Equal Protection Clause of the Fourteenth Amendment. 347 U.S. 483 (1954). A companion case held that segregation in the schools of the District of Columbia violated the due process clause of the Fifth Amendment. Bolling v. Sharpe, 347 U.S. 497 (1954). Subsequent cases have distinguished between *de jure* segregation (created through official state action) and *de facto* segregation (racial imbalance created as a result of other factors, such as residential patterns).

GAO-16-345 Student Diversity

To shed light on this topic, you asked us to explore issues related to the racial and socioeconomic composition of students in K-12 public schools. This report examines (1) how the percentage of schools with high percentages of poor and Black or Hispanic students has changed over time and the characteristics of these schools, (2) why and how selected school districts have implemented actions to increase student diversity, and (3) the extent to which the Departments of Education and Justice have taken actions to identify and address issues related to racial discrimination in schools.

To determine changes in the percentage of schools with specific socioeconomic and racial characteristics over time, we analyzed the Department of Education's (Education) Common Core of Data, a national dataset on all K-12 public schools in the United States. Using this dataset, we analyzed data on schools with different levels of poverty and different levels of Black or Hispanic students from selected school years from 2000-01 to 2013-14, which were the most recent data available.[2] In this report, we used students' eligibility for free or reduced-price lunch as a proxy commonly used to identify poverty levels among schools.[3] We focused on Black and Hispanic students because they are the two largest minority groups in U.S. public schools, and literature shows that these groups experience disparities across a range of areas critical to success in school and the workforce. Further, to compare characteristics of schools with high poverty and high concentrations of Black or Hispanic students to other schools, we analyzed another national Education

_____

[2] Education's Common Core of Data defines "Hispanic or Latino" as a person of Cuban, Mexican, Puerto Rican, South or Central American, or other Spanish culture or origin, regardless of race.

[3] The Department of Agriculture's National School Lunch Program provides low-cost or free lunches to children in schools. Children are eligible for free lunches if their household income is below 130 percent of federal poverty guidelines or if they meet certain automatic eligibility criteria, such as eligibility for the Supplemental Nutrition Assistance Program or Temporary Assistance for Needy Families. Students are eligible for reduced-price lunches if their household income is between 130 percent and 185 percent of federal poverty guidelines. For example, the maximum household income for a family of four to qualify for free lunch benefits was $30,615 in school year 2013-2014. Recent changes in the school lunch program may result in changes in how schools implement the program and thus how they report counts of students eligible for free or reduced-price lunch to Education. These changes could affect data analysis using free or reduced-price lunch eligibility as a proxy for poverty. We do not have evidence that these changes substantively affected our analysis. See appendix I for more information on our methodology.

dataset—the Civil Rights Data Collection—for school year 2011-12.[4] This dataset offered the most recent point-in-time data for all U.S. K-12 public schools for certain data elements, including student characteristics, course offerings, and disciplinary incidents. We determined that the data from both datasets were sufficiently reliable for the purposes of this report by reviewing documentation about the systems used to produce the data, and interviewing Education officials. Our analyses of Education's data in this report are intended to describe selected characteristics of these schools; they should not be used to make conclusions about the presence or absence of unlawful discrimination.

To illustrate why and how selected school districts have taken actions to increase the student diversity of their K-12 public schools, we interviewed (and in two locations visited) officials from one school district in each of three states (one in the Northeast, South, and West). We selected states to include different regions of the country, and we selected school districts within these states that had taken action to increase diversity. We relied on recommendations from subject matter specialists and a review of available information to select school districts. Within these districts, the schools we visited were selected to include a mix of grade level (elementary, middle, and high school), school type (traditional public and magnet), and location (urban and suburban). We interviewed different stakeholders in each district, such as school district superintendents, school board members, state education officials, community leaders, and school officials. While not generalizable to all schools, districts, or to all actions schools could take to diversify, they illustrate a variety of actions districts have taken to increase student diversity.

To describe the actions taken by the Departments of Education and Justice to address issues related to racial discrimination against students in K-12 public schools, we reviewed relevant federal laws, regulations, and agency documents, and interviewed agency officials. We assessed agencies' actions using GAO standards for internal control in the federal government as well as agency guidance and strategic plans. We also discussed school diversity issues with representatives of civil rights organizations and academic subject matter specialists.

---

[4] Consistent with the Common Core of Data, Education's Civil Rights Data Collection defines "Hispanic" or "Latino" as a person of Cuban, Mexican, Puerto Rican, South or Central American, or other Spanish culture or origin, regardless of race.

We conducted this performance audit from November 2014 through April 2016 in accordance with generally accepted government auditing standards. Those standards require that we plan and perform the audit to obtain sufficient, appropriate evidence to provide a reasonable basis for our findings and conclusions based on our audit objectives. We believe that the evidence obtained provides a reasonable basis for our findings and conclusions based on our audit objectives. See appendix I for more detailed information on our scope and methodology.

Background

Federal Civil Rights Laws, School Desegregation Litigation, and the Federal Role

On May 17, 1954, in its *Brown v. Board of Education of Topeka* decision, the United States Supreme Court unanimously held that state laws establishing "separate but equal" public schools for Blacks and Whites were unconstitutional.[5] Ten years after this decision, a relatively small percentage of Black children in the Deep South attended integrated schools. The Civil Rights Act of 1964 prohibited discrimination in schools, employment, and places of public accommodation, and created a new role for federal agencies. Both the Department of Education's (Education) Office for Civil Rights and the Department of Justice's (Justice) Civil Rights Division's Educational Opportunities Section have some responsibility for enforcing Title VI of the Civil Rights Act of 1964, which prohibits discrimination on the basis of race, color, or national origin in programs or activities that receive federal funding, including educational institutions.[6] In addition, Title IV of the Act authorizes Education to provide technical assistance to states or school districts in preparing,

---

[5] 347 U.S. 483 (1954). *Brown* overturned the holding of a prior case, *Plessy v. Ferguson,* that the "separate but equal" doctrine was constitutional. 163 U.S. 537 (1896). In "*Brown II*," the Supreme Court directed the lower courts to fashion remedies to implement its decision "with all deliberate speed." Brown v. Bd. of Educ. of Topeka, 349 U.S. 294 (1955). Years of subsequent desegregation litigation followed, in these and other cases. Review of such case law was beyond the scope of this report.

[6] Specifically, Title VI provides that "[n]o person in the United States shall, on the ground of race, color, or national origin, be excluded from participation in, be denied the benefits of, or be subjected to discrimination under any program or activity receiving Federal financial assistance." Each federal agency that provides federal financial assistance is responsible for ensuring compliance with this requirement. See 42 U.S.C. § 2000d *et seq.* While this report also addresses issues related to socioeconomic status, such status is not a protected class under the U.S. Constitution or any federal civil rights laws.

adopting, and implementing desegregation plans, to arrange for training for school personnel on dealing with educational problems caused by desegregation, and to provide grants to school boards for staff training or hiring specialists to address desegregation.[7] Title IV of the Act also authorizes Justice to file suit in federal court to enforce the civil rights of students in public education,[8] and Title IX of the Act authorizes Justice to intervene—that is, become a party—in federal discrimination lawsuits alleging constitutional violations.[9] Further, Justice has responsibility for enforcing the Equal Educational Opportunities Act of 1974, which among other things, prohibits states from denying equal educational opportunity to individuals, including deliberate segregation of students on the basis of race, color, or national origin.[10]

To aid it in its enforcement and oversight of federal civil rights laws, Education also collects data from school districts about student characteristics and academic offerings, among other things, and compiles these data into a dataset referred to as the Civil Rights Data Collection (or Civil Rights Data). In school year 2011-12, for the first time in about a decade, Education collected these data from all K-12 public schools in the

---

[7] See 42 U.S.C. §§ 2000c-2 to 2000c-4. Through its Title IV Equity Assistance Centers, Education provides technical assistance upon request to applicants in the preparation, adoption, and implementation of desegregation plans. This includes technical assistance to address special educational problems related to desegregation based on race, national origin, or sex.

[8] 42 U.S.C. § 2000c-6.

[9] 42 U.S.C. § 2000h-2. Justice represents the federal government in lawsuits, but for ease of reference in this report we refer to Justice as a party.

[10] See 20 U.S.C. §§ 1701-1758. The Act also prohibits the denial of educational opportunity on the basis of sex. Although outside the scope of this report, the Departments of Education and Justice also enforce the following civil rights laws, which may apply to students in public schools: Title IX of the Educational Amendments Act of 1972, which prohibits discrimination on the basis of sex in any education program or activity receiving federal funds; section 504 of the Rehabilitation Act of 1973, which prohibits discrimination on the basis of disability in any program or activity receiving federal funds; and Title II of the Americans with Disabilities Act of 1990, which prohibits discrimination on the basis of disability by public entities, such as state and local governments. Education also enforces the Boy Scouts of America Equal Access Act, which prohibits public schools, districts, and states that receive Education funding from denying certain youth groups equal access to school facilities for meetings. In addition, under Executive Order 12250, Justice's Federal Coordination and Compliance Section is also responsible for coordinating the implementation and enforcement by federal agencies of various civil rights statutes.

United States.[11] It makes its Civil Rights Data available to the public so that researchers, states, and districts can conduct their own analyses. Beyond its enforcement of federal civil rights laws, Education funds several programs to support diversity in schools. Through its Magnet Schools Assistance Program, Education provides grants to local educational agencies to establish and operate magnet schools that are operated under an eligible desegregation plan.[12] These grants are intended to assist in the desegregation of public schools by supporting the elimination, reduction, and prevention of minority group isolation in elementary and secondary schools with substantial proportions of minority group students. Additionally, through its Excellent Educators of All Initiative, Education launched a 50-state strategy to enforce a statutory provision that required states to take steps to ensure that poor and minority students are not taught by inexperienced, unqualified, or out-of-field teachers at higher rates than other students.[13]

Justice also monitors and enforces the implementation of any open school desegregation court order to which Justice is a party.[14] In court cases where school districts were found to have engaged in segregation or discrimination, courts may issue orders requiring the districts to take specific steps to desegregate their schools or otherwise comply with the law. These "desegregation orders" may include various requirements, such as creating special schools and redrawing attendance zones in such a way as to foster more racial diversity. A federal desegregation order

---

[11] The last time Education collected Civil Rights Data from the universe of K-12 public schools and school districts was in 2000. In previous years, it was collected from a sample of these schools. For the 2012-13 school year, Education has again collected data on all K-12 public schools in the United States and anticipates that these data will be available in June 2016.

[12] Local educational agencies and consortia of local educational agencies may apply for Magnet Schools Assistance Program grants if they operate under a court-ordered or state agency-ordered desegregation plan, a desegregation plan required under Title VI, or a voluntary desegregation plan approved by the Secretary of Education as adequate under Title VI. Not all magnet schools have a desegregative purpose, and not all are funded by the Magnet Schools Assistance Program.

[13] In addition, Education encourages applicants to develop projects that are designed to promote diversity by using this as a priority for selecting grantees in competitive grant programs, such as the Charter School Program.

[14] Litigation may occur in both state and federal courts. Justice is only involved in federal cases and may not be involved in every desegregation or discrimination case at the federal level.

may be lifted when the court determines that the school district has complied in good faith with the order since it was entered and has eliminated all vestiges of past unlawful discrimination to the extent practicable, which is commonly referred to as achieving unitary status.[15] According to Justice officials, the onus is on the school district, not Justice, to seek unitary status because Justice cannot compel a district to ask the court to lift its order. In general, if a district seeks to have a desegregation order lifted, it must file a motion for unitary status with the court. According to information we reviewed, some districts may choose to keep their order in place, even though they have successfully desegregated. Among other things, these orders, according to experts, can help to ensure that schools will not resegregate. Some of the cases that originally ordered districts to desegregate their schools back in the 1960s and 1970s are still open today.[16]

School districts that are not subject to a desegregation order may voluntarily take actions to increase the racial diversity of their schools. Court decisions have also shaped such efforts. For example, in 2007, in *Parents Involved in Community Schools v. Seattle School District No. 1*, the U.S. Supreme Court struck down several school districts' student assignment plans that relied on racial classification.[17] The Court held that the districts failed to show that the use of race in their student assignment plans was necessary to achieve their goal of racial diversity, noting among other things that the racial classifications used had minimal effect on student assignments and that the districts had failed to consider race-neutral alternatives to increase diversity.

Racial and Socioeconomic Demographics of Schools

The composition of the student population in U.S. K-12 public schools has changed significantly over time. In 1975, approximately a decade after enactment of the Civil Rights Act of 1964, Black students were the largest minority group in schools, comprising 14 percent of students and with a

---

[15] In deciding whether a district has achieved unitary status and the desegregation order should be lifted, courts should look not only at student assignments, but to "every facet of school operations—faculty, staff, transportation, extracurricular activities, and facilities." Bd. of Educ. of Oklahoma City Public Schools v. Dowell, 498 U.S. 237, 249-251 (1991) (citing Green v. County Sch. Bd. of New Kent County, 391 U.S. 430, 435 (1969)).

[16] However, the content of a desegregation order may change over time; some districts have been subject to a series of different orders.

[17] 551 U.S. 701 (2007).

poverty rate of about 40 percent.[18] In school year 2013-14, Hispanic students were the largest minority group in schools (25 percent Hispanic students compared to 16 percent Black students), and both groups continue to have poverty rates two to three times higher than the rates of White students. The link between racial and ethnic minorities and poverty is long-standing, as reflected in these data. According to several studies, there is concern about this segment of the population that falls at the intersection of poverty and minority status in schools and how this affects their access to quality education. Of the approximately 93,400 K-12 public schools in the United States, in school year 2013-2014 90 percent of them were traditional schools (which are often located within a neighborhood or community to serve students residing there), 7 percent were charter schools, and 3 percent were magnet schools.

Research on Student Outcomes

An extensive body of research over the past 10 years shows a clear link between schools' socioeconomic (or income) composition and student academic outcomes.[19] That is, the nationally representative studies we reviewed (published from 2004 to 2014) showed that schools with higher concentrations of students from low-income families were generally associated with worse outcomes, and schools with higher concentrations of students from middle- and high-income families were generally associated with better outcomes.[20] For example, one study we reviewed showed that as the average family income of a school increased, the academic achievement and attainment of students of all racial

---

[18] The poverty rates reported in this paragraph apply to children under the age of 18, and the most recent data are as of 2013. See U.S. Department of Education, National Center for Education Statistics, *Digest of Education Statistics*, 2014.

[19] In our selection of studies we defined "income" broadly to include a variety of indicators of family economic well-being such as participation in a free or reduced-price lunch program, as well as family income or indexes that include measures of family members' education, occupation, and income.

[20] We reviewed studies that examined the effect of the racial and income composition of schools' student bodies on the academic outcomes of students in those schools. These studies used nationally representative samples of schools and students and methods that controlled for multiple factors that may affect student outcomes. One study included in our review found that students from low-income families attending school with higher-income peers had lower math and science scores than students from low-income families attending predominantly low-income schools. See appendix I for more information about our study review. See appendix III for a list of studies included in our review.

backgrounds increased.[21] The converse was also true. For example, another study found that students attending schools with lower average family income learned at a slower pace than students attending schools where income was higher.[22]

The studies, however, paint a more nuanced picture of the effects of schools' racial composition on student academic outcomes. Specifically, while some of the studies found that having higher percentages of Black or Hispanic students resulted in weaker student outcomes, those effects were often confounded by other factors, including family income, and sometimes the racial composition of schools affected students differently. For example, one study concluded that the average family income of a school had a stronger and more negative effect on academic outcomes, but it also found that, after controlling for other factors, as the percentage of minority students increased in a school, Hispanic students were more likely to graduate from high school, and Asian students were less likely to graduate compared to White students.[23] In another example, a 2010 study found that, after controlling for characteristics such as average family income in the neighborhood, the percentage of Black students in a school had no effect on the likelihood of high school graduation for students of all racial groups and had a small positive effect for all students' chances of earning a bachelor's degree.[24] See appendix III for the list of studies we reviewed.

---

[21] Igor Ryabov, "Adolescent Academic Outcomes in School Context: Network Effects Reexamined," *Journal of Adolescence*, vol. 34 (2011).

[22] Gregory J. Palardy, "Differential School Effects Among Low, Middle, and High Social Class Composition Schools: A Multiple Group, Multilevel Latent Growth Curve Analysis," *School Effectiveness and School Improvement: An International Journal of Research, Policy and Practice,* vol. 19, no. 1 (2008).

[23] Ryabov, "Adolescent Academic Outcomes," 923-925.

[24] Ann Owens, "Neighborhoods and Schools as Competing and Reinforcing Contexts for Educational Attainment," *Sociology of Education*, vol. 83, no. 4 (2010).

The Percentage of High-Poverty Schools with Mostly Black or Hispanic Students Increased over Time, and Such Schools Tend to Have Fewer Resources

High-Poverty Schools with Mostly Black or Hispanic Students Represent 16 Percent of All K-12 Public Schools

Over time, there has been a large increase in schools that are the most isolated by poverty and race. From school years 2000-01 to 2013-14 (most recent data available), both the percentage of K-12 public schools that were high poverty and comprised of mostly Black or Hispanic students (H/PBH) and the students attending these schools grew significantly. In these schools 75 to 100 percent of the students were eligible for free or reduced-price lunch, and 75 to 100 percent of the students were Black or Hispanic.[25] As shown in figure 1, the percentage of H/PBH schools out of all K-12 public schools increased steadily from 9 percent in 2000-01 (7,009 schools) to 16 percent in 2013-14 (15,089 schools).[26] See table 3 in appendix II for data separately breaking out these schools by the percent that are majority Black students and the percent that are majority Hispanic students. While H/PBH schools represented 16 percent of all K-12 public schools, they represented 61 percent of all high-poverty schools in 2013-14. See table 4 in appendix II for additional information on high-poverty schools.

---

[25] In this report, unless otherwise indicated, we grouped schools into three categories based on the percentage of students who were eligible for free or reduced-price school lunch as well as the percentage of students who were Black or Hispanic. The groups are as follows: (1) schools in which 75 to 100 percent of the students were eligible for free or reduced-price school lunch and 75 to 100 percent of the students were Black or Hispanic (referred to as H/PBH schools), (2) schools in which 0 to 25 percent of the students were eligible for free or reduced-price school lunch and 0 to 25 percent of the students were Black or Hispanic (referred to as L/PBH schools), and (3) all other schools—those schools that fall outside of these two categories. See appendix I for more information.

[26] For information presented in the text, figures, and tables, we computed all calculations based on Education's data.

Further, at the other end of the spectrum, the percentage of schools that were low poverty and comprised of fewer Black or Hispanic students (L/PBH) decreased by almost half over this same time period.[27] In L/PBH schools, 0 to 25 percent of the students were eligible for free or reduced-priced lunch, and 0 to 25 percent were Black or Hispanic.

Figure 1: Changes in the Percentage of High-Poverty Schools Comprised of Mostly Black or Hispanic Students, Selected School Years from 2000-01 to 2013-14

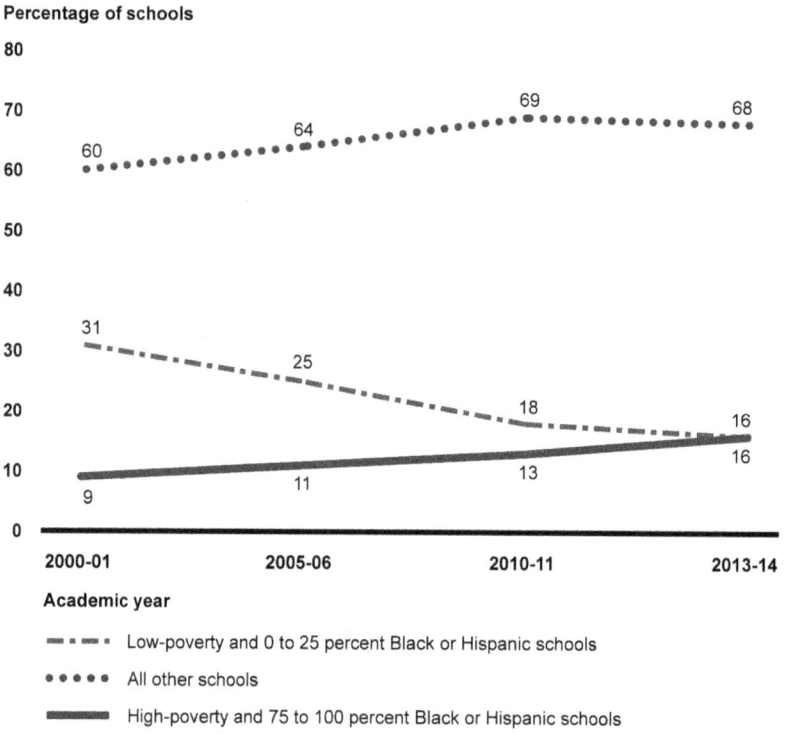

Source: GAO analysis of Department of Education, Common Core of Data, 2000-14. | GAO-16-345

Notes: "Low-poverty" refers to schools in which 0 to 25 percent of the students were eligible for free or reduced-price lunch. "High-poverty" refers to schools in which 75 to 100 percent of the students were eligible for free or reduced-price lunch. "All other schools" refers to schools that fall outside of the other two categories of schools in this figure. This figure excludes schools that did not report (1) free or reduced-price school lunch, which we used as a proxy to categorize the poverty level of the school or (2) the number of Black or Hispanic students, which we used to categorize the level of Black or Hispanic students in the school.

---

[27] As figure 1 shows, over this same time period, the percentage of all other schools (i.e., schools that fall outside of the L/PBH and H/PBH categories) increased by 8 percentage points.

GAO-16-345 Student Diversity

In addition, more students are attending H/PBH schools than in the past. As shown in figure 2, the number of students attending H/PBH schools more than doubled, increasing by about 4.3 million students, from about 4.1 million to 8.4 million students (or from 10 percent to 17 percent of all K-12 public school students).[28] Also, the percentage of Hispanic students is higher than that of Black students in these schools.[29] Hispanic students tend to be "triply segregated" by race, income, and language, according to subject matter specialists we interviewed and, according to Education data, are the largest minority group in K-12 public schools. The U.S. Census Bureau projects that by 2044, minorities will be the majority in the United States.

Further, among H/PBH schools, there is a subset of schools with even higher percentages of poverty and Black or Hispanic students, and growth in these schools has been dramatic. Specifically, according to our analysis of Education's data, the number of schools where 90 to 100 percent of the students were eligible for free or reduced-price lunch and 90 to 100 percent of the students were Black or Hispanic grew by 143 percent from school years 2000-01 to 2013-14. In school year 2013-14, these schools represented 6 percent of all K-12 public schools, and 6 percent of students attended them (see appendix II for additional information on this subset of schools).

---

[28] As figure 2 shows, over this same time period, the number of students attending L/PBH schools decreased, and the number of students attending all other schools increased.

[29] From school year 2000-01 to 2013-14, in H/PBH schools, Hispanic students grew from 48 to 58 percent, and Black students decreased from 45 to 34 percent, although there was an absolute increase in the number of Black students.

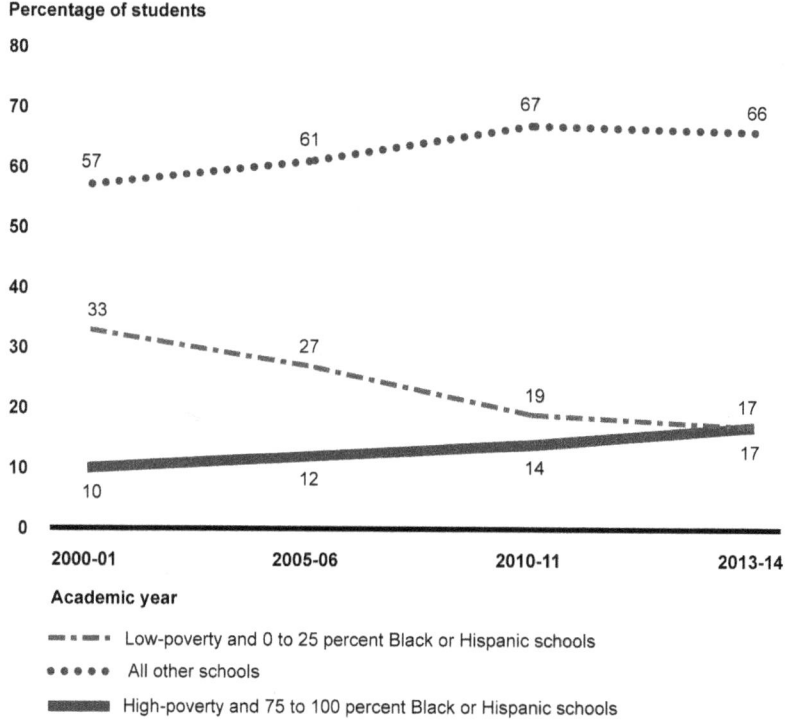

Figure 2: Changes in the Percentage of Students Who Attend High-Poverty Schools of Mostly Black or Hispanic Students Compared to the Percentage of Students Who Attend Other Schools, Selected School Years from 2000-01 to 2013-14

Percentage of students

- - · - · Low-poverty and 0 to 25 percent Black or Hispanic schools
· · · · · All other schools
▬▬▬ High-poverty and 75 to 100 percent Black or Hispanic schools

Source: GAO analysis of Department of Education, Common Core of Data, 2000-14. | GAO-16-345

Notes: "Low-poverty" refers to schools in which 0 to 25 percent of the students were eligible for free or reduced-price lunch. "High-poverty" refers to schools in which 75 to 100 percent of the students were eligible for free or reduced-price lunch. "All other schools" refers to schools that fall outside of the other two categories of schools in this figure. This figure excludes schools that did not report (1) free or reduced-price school lunch, which we used as a proxy to categorize the poverty level of the school or (2) the number of Black or Hispanic students, which we used to categorize the level of Black or Hispanic students in the school.

H/PBH schools are largely traditional schools; however, the percentage of H/PBH schools that are traditional schools decreased from 94 percent to 81 percent from school years 2000-01 to 2013-14. In contrast, the percentage of such schools that were charter schools and magnet schools increased over that time period from 3 percent to 13 percent and from 3 percent to 5 percent, respectively (see fig. 3). In addition, with respect to the socioeconomic and racial composition of charter schools and magnet schools, both are disproportionately H/PBH schools. For example, in 2013-14, 13 percent of H/PBH schools were charter schools, while 5 percent of L/PBH schools were charter schools. To comply with federal law, some districts may have converted low-performing public schools to charter schools, which may have contributed, in part, to the growth among high-poverty and minority populations in charter schools.[30] Further, 5 percent of H/PBH schools were magnet schools, while 2 percent of L/PBH schools were magnet schools.

Figure 3: Changes in Percentage of High-Poverty Schools of Mostly Black or Hispanic Students, by School Type, School Years 2000-01 and 2013-14

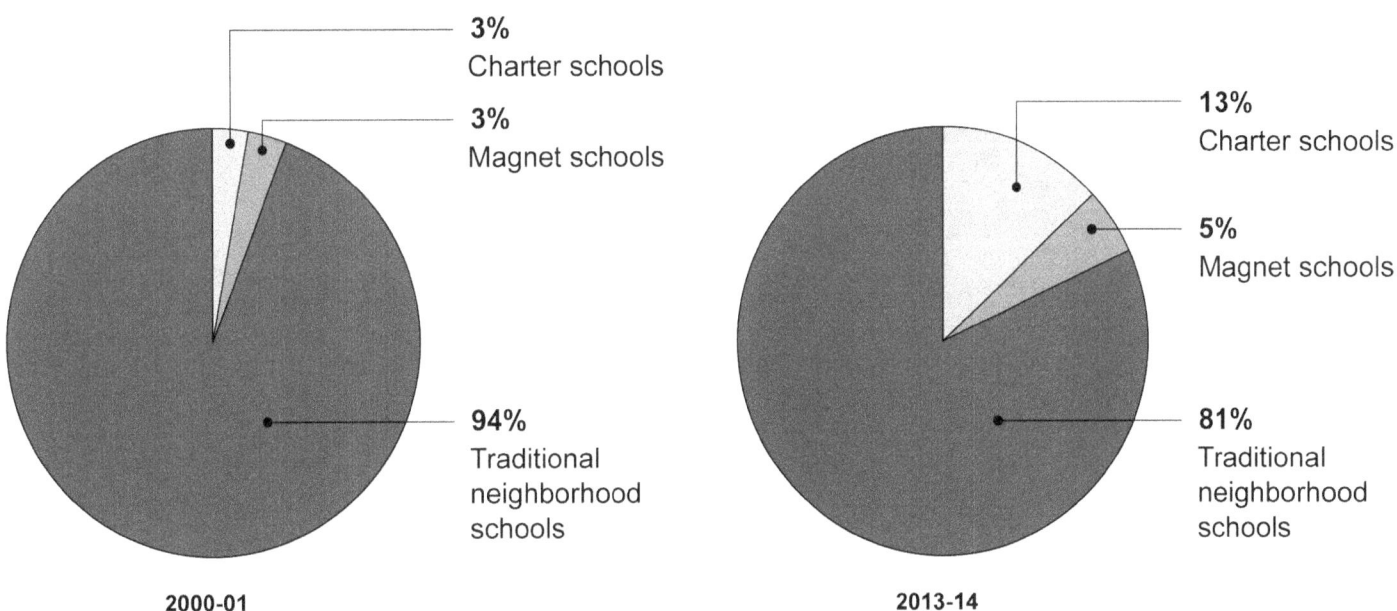

3% Charter schools

3% Magnet schools

94% Traditional neighborhood schools

2000-01

13% Charter schools

5% Magnet schools

81% Traditional neighborhood schools

2013-14

Source: GAO analysis of Department of Education, Common Core of Data, 2000-01 and 2013-14. | GAO-16-345

Notes: "High-poverty schools of Mostly Black or Hispanic Students" refers to schools in which 75 to 100 percent of the students were eligible for free or reduced-price lunch and 75 to 100 percent of the students were Black or Hispanic. This figure excludes schools that did not report (1) free or reduced-price school lunch, which we used as a proxy to categorize the poverty level of the school or (2) the number of Black or Hispanic students, which we used to categorize the level of Black or Hispanic students in the school.

[30] To receive federal funding under Title I of the Elementary and Secondary Education Act of 1965, as amended by the No Child Left Behind Act of 2001, states and districts are required to implement various requirements. For schools that fail to meet specified academic progress benchmarks, districts were required to implement certain interventions, which may include, among other things, reopening the school as a public charter school. 20 U.S.C. §§ 6311, 6316. In December 2015, the Every Student Succeeds Act was enacted, which eliminates these requirements and creates new requirements for school support and improvement, most of which will take effect at the beginning of school year 2017-18. Pub. L. No. 114-95, 129 Stat. 1802 (2015).

GAO-16-345 Student Diversity

In terms of school type, the percentage of students who attended H/PBH schools decreased for traditional schools but increased among charter and magnet schools. For traditional schools the percentage of students dropped from 95 percent to 83 percent, even though there was an absolute increase in the number of students at H/PBH traditional schools (from 3.9 million to 6.9 million students, according to our analysis of Education's data). The percentage of students who attended H/PBH charter schools increased from 1 percent to 9 percent (55,477 to 795,679 students), and those who attended H/PBH magnet schools increased from 4 percent to 8 percent (152,592 to 667,834) (see fig. 4).

Figure 4: Changes in Percentage of Students Who Attend High-Poverty Schools Comprised of Mostly Black or Hispanic Students, by School Type, School Years 2000-01 and 2013-14

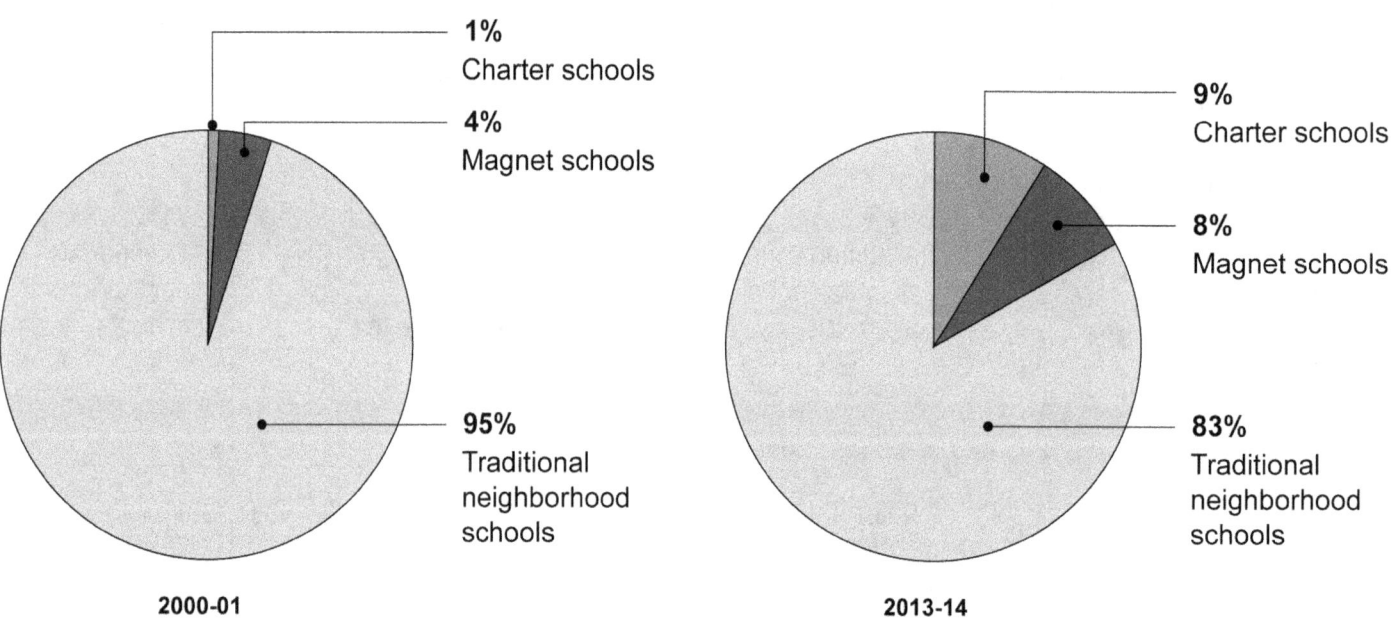

1%
Charter schools

4%
Magnet schools

95%
Traditional neighborhood schools

2000-01

9%
Charter schools

8%
Magnet schools

83%
Traditional neighborhood schools

2013-14

Source: GAO analysis of Department of Education, Common Core of Data, 2000-01 and 2013-14. | GAO-16-345

Notes: "High-poverty schools of Mostly Black or Hispanic Students" refers to schools in which 75 to 100 percent of the students were eligible for free or reduced-price lunch and 75 to 100 percent of the students were Black or Hispanic. This figure excludes schools that did not report (1) free or reduced-price school lunch, which we used as a proxy to categorize the poverty level of the school or (2) the number of Black or Hispanic students, which we used to categorize the level of Black or Hispanic students in the school.

High-Poverty Schools with Mostly Black or Hispanic Students Generally Have Fewer Resources and More Disciplinary Actions Than Other Schools

Research shows that lower levels of income were generally associated with worse student educational outcomes (see app. III). Our analysis of Education data also showed that schools that were highly isolated by poverty and race generally had fewer resources and disproportionately more disciplinary actions than other schools. As shown in figures 5 through 9, when comparing H/PBH schools to L/PBH schools and all other schools (i.e., schools that fall outside of these two categories), disparities existed across a range of areas in school year 2011-12, the most recent year for which these data were available.[31] Further, disparities were even greater for the subset of H/PBH schools in which 90 to 100 percent of the students were eligible for free or reduced-price lunch and 90 to 100 percent of the students were Black or Hispanic, across most areas analyzed. In addition, comparing just the H/PBH traditional, charter, and magnet schools, we also found differences. (See app. II for additional data, including data comparing schools in which 90 to 100 percent of the students were eligible for free or reduced-price lunch and 90 to 100 percent of the students were Black or Hispanic to other schools). As previously mentioned, although our analyses of Education's data showed disparities across a range of different areas, these analyses, taken alone, should not be used to make conclusions about the presence or absence of unlawful discrimination.

The Importance of Middle School Algebra, STEM courses, and AP and GATE Programs

Several academic courses and programs are especially beneficial in preparing students for college and successful careers. Among these are middle school algebra; courses in Science, Technology, Engineering, and Mathematics (STEM) fields; Advanced Placement (AP) courses; and Gifted and Talented Education (GATE) programs. According to the Department of Education, access to algebra in middle school—that is, in 7th or 8th grade—positions students to complete higher-level courses in math and science in high school, which is critical to preparing students for college and careers. Therefore, access to a full range of STEM courses in high school, such as calculus, chemistry, and physics, is important in preparing students for college and careers in high-demand fields. In addition, rigorous academic programs, such as AP and GATE, can improve student achievement and build skills that help students move toward college- and career-readiness. AP courses help prepare high school students for college-level courses and upon passing the AP exam, may enable students to receive college credit.

Source: U.S. Department of Education, Office for Civil Rights, Protecting Civil Rights, Advancing Equity: Report to the President and Secretary of Education, Under Section 203(b)(1) of the Department of Education Organization Act, FY 13-14, April 2015; U.S. Department of Education, Office for Civil Rights, Dear Colleague Letter: Resource Comparability, October 2014; and U.S. Department of Education, Office for Civil Rights, Civil Rights Data Collection: Data Snapshot (College and Career Readiness), March 2014. | GAO-16-345

---

[31] For additional data available in Education's Civil Rights Data Collection for school year 2011-12 not included in this report, see http://ocrdata.ed.gov/downloads/FAQ.pdf.

Academic and College Preparatory Courses

According to our analysis of Education's data, lower percentages of H/PBH schools offered a range of math courses, with differences greatest for 7th or 8th grade algebra and calculus, and differences less evident for algebra II and geometry compared to L/PBH schools and all other schools (see fig. 5).[32] According to Education, access to algebra in 7th or 8th grade positions students to complete higher-level courses in math and science in high school, which is critical to preparing students for college and careers. Among just the H/PBH schools, a higher percentage of magnet schools offered these four math courses. Between just H/PBH traditional schools and charter schools, a higher percentage of traditional schools offered 7h or 8th grade algebra and calculus, while a higher percentage of charter schools offered algebra II and geometry (see app. II for additional data).

---

[32] This analysis looked at whether schools with 7th grade or higher (which included some K-8 schools in addition to middle schools and high schools) offered algebra in 7th or 8th grade, algebra II, geometry, and calculus. Further, our analyses based on the Civil Rights Data is for school year 2011-12 (the most recent available at the time of our analysis) and our analysis of CCD is for school years 2000-01, 2005-06, 2010-11, and 2013-14 (the most recent available at the time of our analysis). Therefore, the numbers and percentages of schools and students derived from these two sets of data will not match. See appendix 1 for our scope and methodology.

Figure 5: Percentage of Middle and High Schools Offering Selected Math Courses, School Year 2011-12

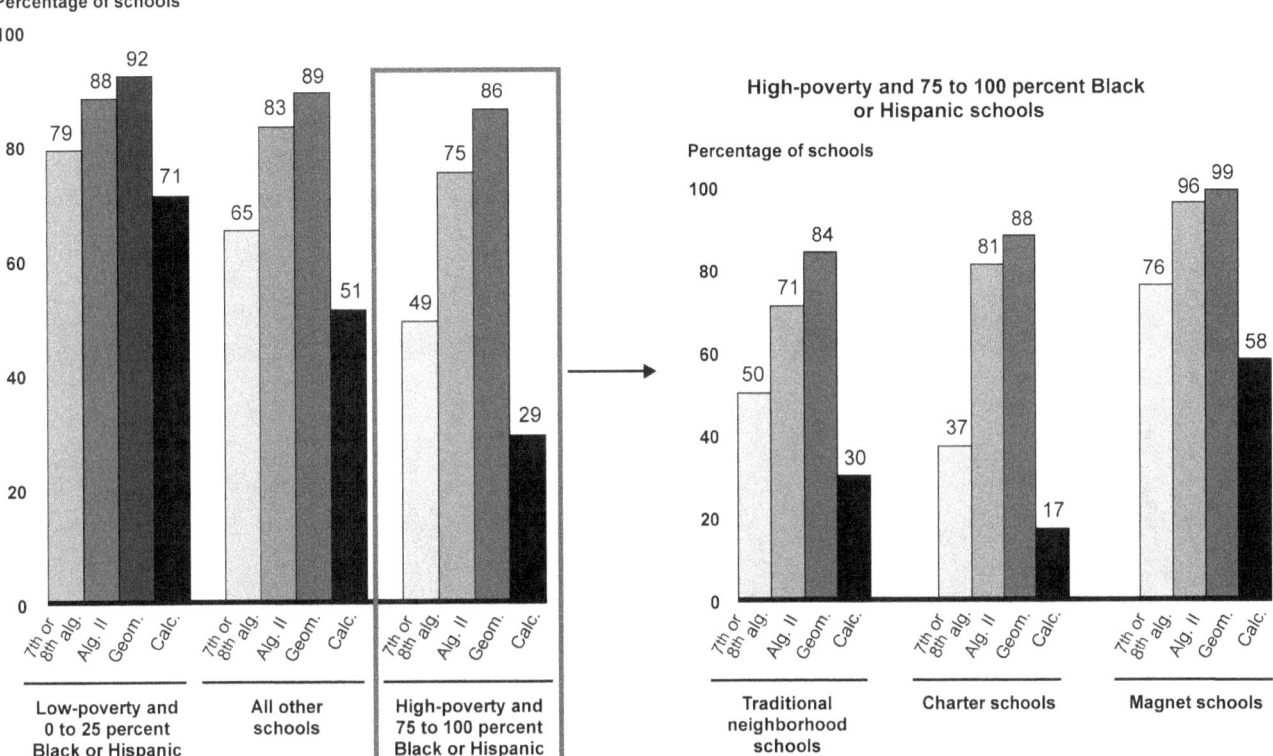

7th or 8th alg. = 7th or 8th grade algebra
Alg. II = Algebra II
Geom. = Geometry
Calc. = Calculus

Source: GAO analysis of Department of Education, Civil Rights Data Collection, 2011-12. | GAO-16-345

Notes: "Low-poverty" refers to schools in which 0 to 25 percent of the students were eligible for free or reduced-price lunch. "High-poverty" refers to schools in which 75 to 100 percent of the students were eligible for free or reduced-price lunch. "All other schools" refers to schools that fall outside of the other two categories of schools in this figure. This figure is based on analysis of schools with 7th grade or higher, and includes some K-8 schools in addition to middle schools and high schools. This figure excludes schools that did not report whether they offered the course. For this analysis we matched schools in the Civil Rights Data for school year 2011-12 to schools in the Common Core of Data for school year 2011-12 and excluded schools for which there was not a match. We also excluded schools that did not report (1) free or reduced-price school lunch, which we used as a proxy to categorize the poverty level of the school and (2) the number of Black or Hispanic students, which we used to categorize the level of Black or Hispanic students in the school.

Similarly, with respect to science courses—biology, chemistry, and physics—our analyses of Education data show disparities, with a lower percentage of H/PBH schools offering these courses compared to L/PBH schools and all other schools, with differences most evident for physics. Among just the H/PBH schools, a higher percentage of magnet schools offered all three science courses. Between just H/PBH traditional schools and charter schools, a higher percentage of charter schools offered biology and chemistry (see fig. 6).[33]

Figure 6: Percentage of Middle and High Schools Offering Selected Science Courses, School Year 2011-12

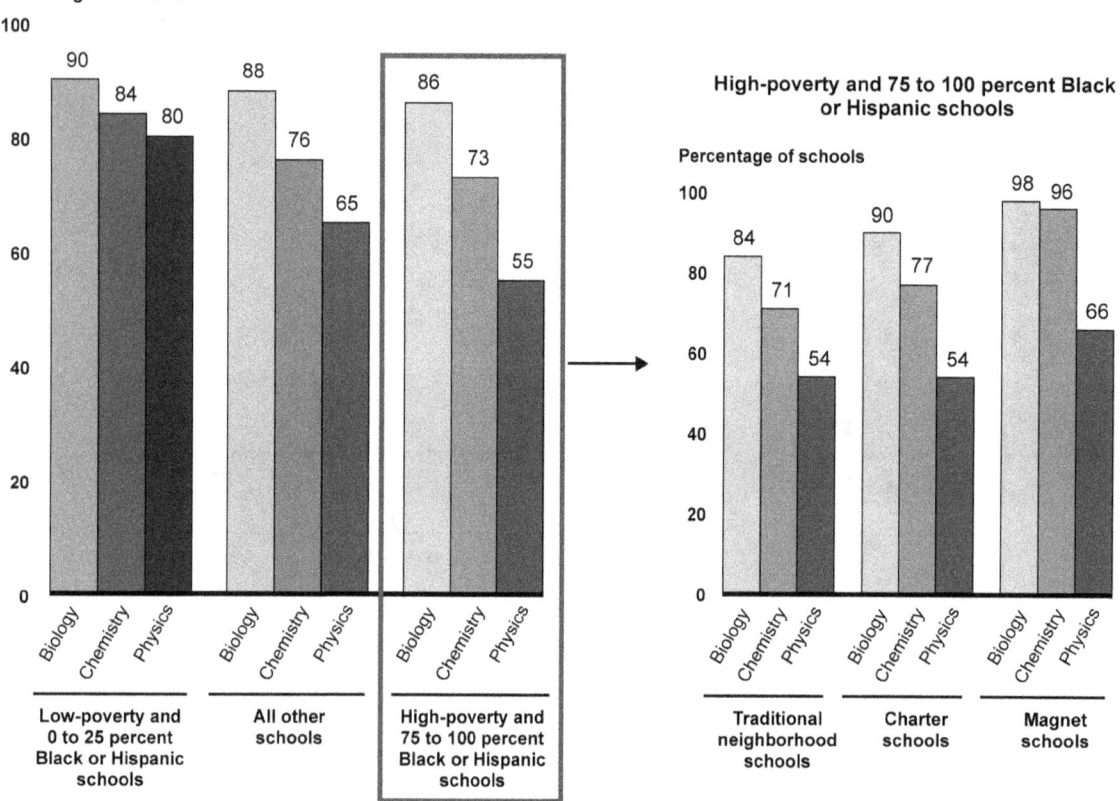

Source: GAO analysis of Department of Education, Civil Rights Data Collection, 2011-12. | GAO-16-345

Notes: "Low-poverty" refers to schools in which 0 to 25 percent of the students were eligible for free or reduced-price lunch. "High-poverty" refers to schools in which 75 to 100 percent of the students were eligible for free or reduced-price lunch. "All other schools" refers to schools that fall outside of the other two categories of schools in this figure. This figure is based on analysis of schools with 7th grade or higher, and includes some K-8 schools in addition to middle schools and high schools. This figure excludes schools that did not report whether they offered the course. For this analysis we matched schools in the Civil Rights Data for school year 2011-12 to schools in the Common Core of Data for school year 2011-12 and excluded schools for which there was not a match. We also

[33] Between just H/PBH traditional schools and charter schools, the same percentage of schools offered physics (54 percent), with a higher percentage of magnet schools offering physics (66 percent).

excluded schools that did not report (1) free or reduced-price school lunch, which we used as a proxy to categorize the poverty level of the school and (2) the number of Black or Hispanic students, which we used to categorize the level of Black or Hispanic students in the school.

With respect to AP courses,[34] there were also disparities, as a lower percentage of H/PBH schools offered these courses compared to L/PBH schools and all other schools. Differences were the greatest between H/PBH schools (48 percent of these schools offered AP courses) and L/PBH schools (72 percent of these schools offered these courses). Among just the H/PBH schools, a higher percentage of magnet schools (83 percent) offered AP courses than did the traditional schools (50 percent) or charter schools (32 percent) (see fig. 7). In addition, among schools that offered AP courses, a lower percentage of students of all racial groups (Black, Hispanic, White, Asian, and Other) attending H/PBH schools took AP courses compared to students of all racial groups in L/PBH schools and all other schools. Specifically, among schools that offered AP courses, 12 percent of all students attending H/PBH schools took an AP course compared to 24 percent of all students in L/PBH schools and 17 percent of all students in all other schools.[35]

In addition, with respect to Gifted and Talented Education programs, or GATE,[36] a lower percentage of H/PBH schools offered these programs compared to all other schools; however, a higher percentage of H/PBH schools offered GATE programs compared to L/PBH schools. Looking at just H/PBH schools, almost three-quarters of magnet schools and almost

---

[34] According to Education, AP is a rigorous academic program that can improve student achievement and build skills that help students move toward college- and career-readiness.

[35] This analysis is based on the percentage of students enrolling in at least one AP course.

[36] GATE programs are offered during regular school hours to students because of unusually high academic ability or aptitude or a specialized talent or aptitude.

two-thirds of traditional schools offered this program, while less than one-fifth of charter schools offered it (see fig. 7).[37]

Figure 7: Percentage of Schools Offering Advanced Placement (AP) Courses and Gifted and Talented Education (GATE) Programs, School Year 2011-12

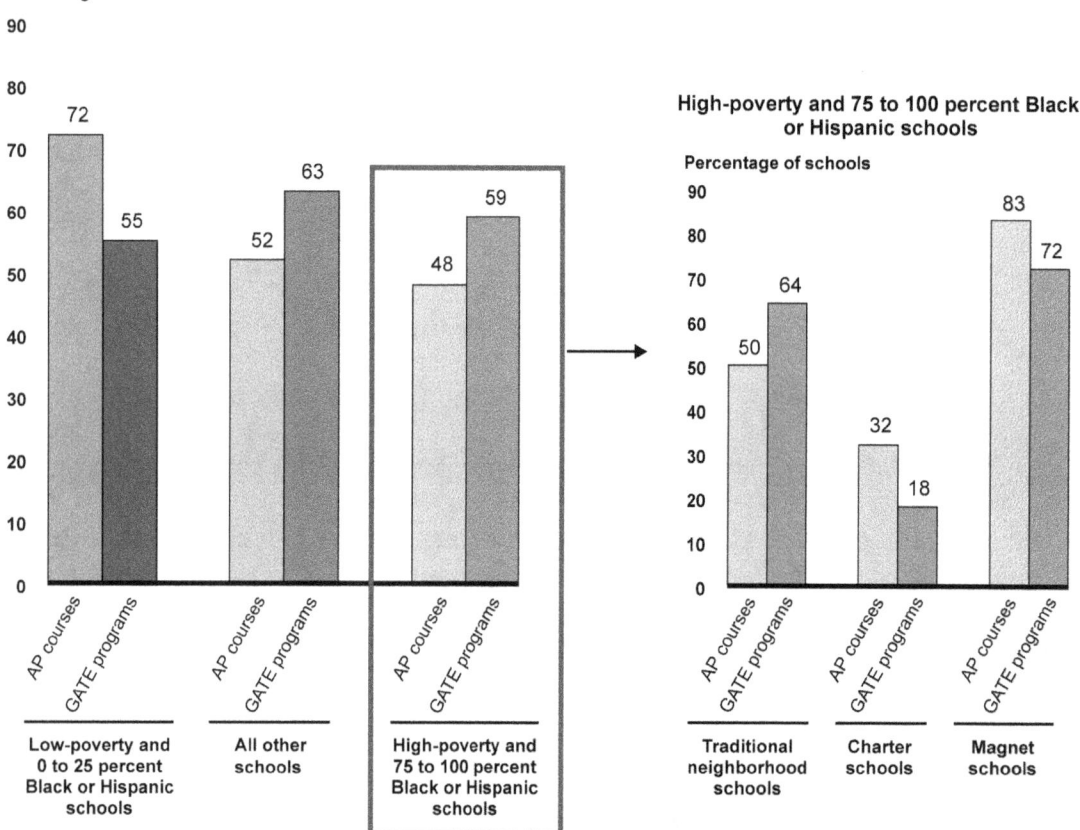

Source: GAO analysis of Department of Education, Civil Rights Data Collection, 2011-12. | GAO-16-345

Notes: "Low-poverty" refers to schools in which 0 to 25 percent of the students were eligible for free or reduced-price lunch. "High-poverty" refers to schools in which 75 to 100 percent of the students

---

[37] Education's Civil Rights Data Collection also contains data on the International Baccalaureate (IB) Diploma Programme (see http://ocrdata.ed.gov/downloads/FAQ.pdf for data on the IB Diploma Programme for school year 2011-12). The IB Diploma Programme, sponsored by the International Baccalaureate Organization, was designed to be an academically challenging and balanced program of education with final examinations that prepares students, normally aged 16 to 19, for success at university and life beyond. Further, a significantly lower percentage of schools offer IB Programme's compared to AP courses, according to the IB Diploma Programme and the College Board.

were eligible for free or reduced-price lunch. "All other schools" refers to schools that fall outside of the other two categories of schools in this figure. This figure is based on analysis of schools with any grades between 9th and 12th grade for AP courses and analysis of all schools for GATE programs. This figure excludes schools that did not report whether they offered the course. For this analysis we matched schools in the Civil Rights Data for school year 2011-12 to schools in the Common Core of Data for school year 2011-12 and excluded schools for which there was not a match. We also excluded schools that did not report (1) free or reduced-price school lunch, which we used as a proxy to categorize the poverty level of the school and (2) the number of Black or Hispanic students, which we used to categorize the level of Black or Hispanic students in the school.

The Effect of School Discipline Policies

According to the Department of Education, discipline policies and practices that remove students from engaging instruction—such as suspensions, expulsions, and referrals to law enforcement—generally fail to help students improve their behavior and fail to improve school safety. Specifically, students who receive out-of-school suspensions are excluded from school for disciplinary reasons for one school day or longer and lose important instructional time, and suspended students are less likely to graduate on time and more likely to repeat a grade, drop out of school, and become involved in the juvenile justice system. Black students are also overrepresented among students receiving disciplinary actions, beginning as early as preschool, according to Education.

Source: U.S. Department of Education, Office of Elementary and Secondary Education, Rethink School Discipline: School District Leader Summit on Improving School Climate and Discipline, Resource Guide for Superintendent Action, July 2015; U.S. Department of Education, Office for Civil Rights, Civil Rights Data Collection: Data Snapshot (School Discipline), March 2014; and U.S. Department of Justice, Civil Rights Division and U.S. Department of Education, Office for Civil Rights, Dear Colleague Letter on Nondiscriminatory Administration of School Discipline, January 2014. | GAO-16-345

Student Retention and Discipline

Students in H/PBH schools were held back in 9th grade, suspended (out-of-school), and expelled at disproportionately higher rates than students in L/PBH schools and all other schools. Specifically, although students in H/PBH schools were 7 percent of all 9th grade students, they were 17 percent of all students retained in 9th grade, according to our analysis of Education's data (see fig. 8).[38] Further, with respect to suspensions and expulsions, there was a similar pattern. Specifically, although students in H/PBH schools accounted for 12 percent of all students, they represented 22 percent of all students with one or more out-of-school suspensions and 16 percent of all students expelled (see fig. 9 and fig. 10). For additional information comparing students in schools with different levels of Black, Hispanic, and poor students, and by school type (traditional, charter, and magnet schools), see tables 20 and 21 in appendix II.

---

[38] This analysis was based on only those schools with 9th grade.

Figure 8: Percentage of Students Retained in 9th Grade, School Year 2011-12

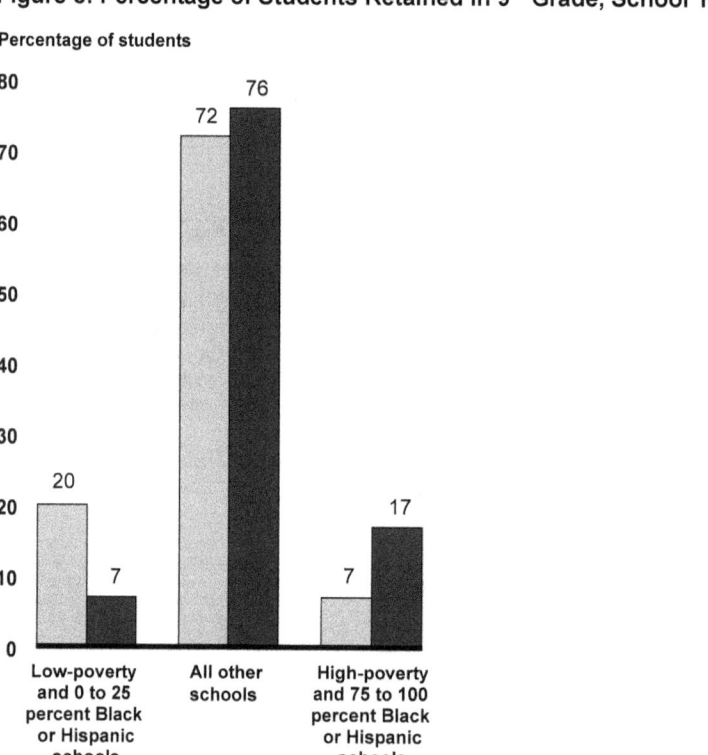

Source: GAO analysis of Department of Education, Civil Rights Data Collection, 2011-12. | GAO-16-345

Notes: "Low-poverty" refers to schools in which 0 to 25 percent of the students were eligible for free or reduced-price lunch. "High-poverty" refers to schools in which 75 to 100 percent of the students were eligible for free or reduced-price lunch. "All other schools" refers to schools that fall outside of the other two categories of schools in this figure. This figure is based on analysis of schools with 9th grade. This figure excludes schools that did not report whether they retained students. For this analysis we matched schools in the Civil Rights Data for school year 2011-12 to schools in the Common Core of Data for school year 2011-12 and excluded schools for which there was not a match. We also excluded schools that did not report (1) free or reduced-price school lunch, which we used as a proxy to categorize the poverty level of the school and (2) the number of Black or Hispanic students, which we used to categorize the level of Black or Hispanic students in the school.

Figure 9: Percentage of Students with More than One Out-of-School Suspension, School Year 2011-12

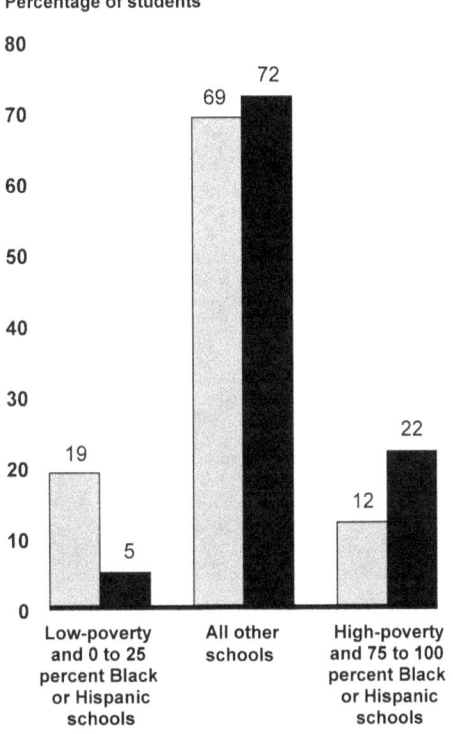

Percentage of students

Total students in these schools

Students with more than one out-of-school suspension

Source: GAO analysis of Department of Education, Civil Rights Data Collection, 2011-12. | GAO-16-345

Notes: "Low-poverty" refers to schools in which 0 to 25 percent of the students were eligible for free or reduced-price lunch. "High-poverty" refers to schools in which 75 to 100 percent of the students were eligible for free or reduced-price lunch. "All other schools" refers to schools that fall outside of the other two categories of schools in this figure. This figure excludes schools that did not report whether they suspended students. For this analysis we matched schools in the Civil Rights Data for school year 2011-12 to schools in the Common Core of Data for school year 2011-12 and excluded schools for which there was not a match. We also excluded schools that did not report (1) free or reduced-price school lunch, which we used as a proxy to categorize the poverty level of the school and (2) the number of Black or Hispanic students, which we used to categorize the level of Black or Hispanic students in the school.

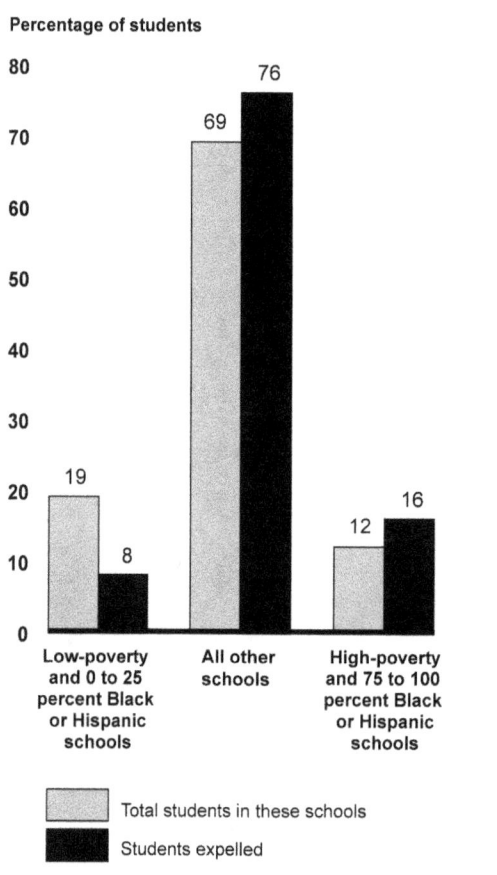

Figure 10: Percentage of Students Expelled, School Year 2011-12

Percentage of students

	Total students in these schools	Students expelled
Low-poverty and 0 to 25 percent Black or Hispanic schools	19	8
All other schools	69	76
High-poverty and 75 to 100 percent Black or Hispanic schools	12	16

Source: GAO analysis of Department of Education, Civil Rights Data Collection, 2011-12. | GAO-16-345

Notes: "Low-poverty" refers to schools in which 0 to 25 percent of the students were eligible for free or reduced-price lunch. "High-poverty" refers to schools in which 75 to 100 percent of the students were eligible for free or reduced-price lunch. "All other schools" refers to schools that fall outside of the other two categories of schools in this figure. This figure excludes schools that did not report whether they expelled students. For this analysis we matched schools in the Civil Rights Data for school year 2011-12 to schools in the Common Core of Data for school year 2011-12 and excluded schools for which there was not a match. We also excluded schools that did not report (1) free or reduced-price school lunch, which we used as a proxy to categorize the poverty level of the school and (2) the number of Black or Hispanic students, which we used to categorize the level of Black or Hispanic students in the school.

English Learners and Students with Disabilities

H/PBH schools have large percentages of Hispanic students and, as expected, have a disproportionately greater percentage of students who were English Learners (EL). With respect to students with disabilities, our analysis of Education's data showed small differences across two of the school groupings we analyzed. Specifically, L/PBH schools had 19 percent of all students and 17 of the students with disabilities, and all other schools had 69 percent of all students and 71 percent of the students with disabilities, according to our analysis of Education's data. Further, while these comparisons show some slight differences *by school* in the percent of students with disabilities, Education's own analysis of these data *by race* showed there are differences among racial groups, with Black students overall being overrepresented among students with disabilities.[39]

To Address Racial Imbalances and Demographic Shifts, Selected Districts Reported Taking Various Actions to Increase Diversity of Schools

Because their schools were largely isolated by race and poverty or had experienced large demographic shifts, the three school districts we reviewed—located in the Northeast, South, and West—reported implementing a variety of actions in an effort to increase racial and socioeconomic diversity in their schools.[40] However, in implementing these efforts aimed at increasing diversity, school districts struggled with providing transportation to students and obtaining support from parents and the community, among other things.

School District in the Northeast. The district in the Northeast, an urban, predominantly low-income, Black and Hispanic district surrounded by primarily White suburban districts, had tried for over two decades to diversify its schools, according to state officials. Despite these efforts, continued racial isolation and poverty among schools in the district prompted a group of families to file a lawsuit against the state in state court, alleging that the education students received in the urban district was inferior to that received in the more affluent, largely White suburban schools. The plaintiffs argued that the state's system of separate city and suburban school districts, which had been in place almost a century, led to racially segregated schools. The state supreme court ruled that the conditions in the district violated the state constitution, requiring the state

---

[39] According to Education, in 2013 American Indian or Alaska Native, Black or African American, and Native Hawaiian or Other Pacific Islander students aged 6 through 21 were more likely to be categorized as students with disabilities (i.e., served under the Individuals with Disabilities Education Act, part B) than were students aged 6 through 21 in all other racial/ethnic groups combined. See Department of Education, Office of Special Education and Rehabilitative Services, *37th Annual Report to the Congress on the Implementation of the Individuals with Disabilities Education Act, 2015* (December 2015).

[40] In this report, our descriptions of the three selected districts are intended only to illustrate some of the actions districts have taken to improve diversity of their schools. We did not assess the extent to which the selected districts have achieved their diversity goals or complied with any applicable court orders.

to take action to diversify the urban district and its surrounding suburban schools.[41]

In response, the state and district took a variety of actions. In particular the state provided funding to build several new or completely renovated state-of-the-art magnet schools within the region to attract suburban students. To attract students from the city and suburbs, the magnet schools used highly specialized curriculum. For example, one newly renovated environmental sciences magnet school we visited offered theme-based instruction that allowed students to work side-by-side with resident scientists to conduct investigations and studies using a variety of technologies and tools. Other magnet schools in this area offered different themes, such as aerospace and engineering or the performing arts. To further facilitate its efforts at diversity, the state provided funding for transportation to magnet schools, enabling suburban and urban students to more easily attend these schools. In addition, according to officials, consistent with the court order, the state required the district's magnet schools to maintain a student enrollment of no more than 75 percent minority students.

However, the district faced several challenges with respect to its magnet schools. For example, officials said maintaining a certain ratio of non-minority students posed challenges. According to the district superintendent, even if there were openings, many minority students in the district were unable to attend certain magnet schools because doing so would interfere with the ratio of minorities to non-minorities the state was attempting to achieve. In addition, because assignment to magnet schools was done through a lottery, students were not guaranteed a slot in a magnet school. Officials told us that in those cases where there was not enough space in a magnet school or where admitting more minority students would disrupt the ratio of minorities to non-minorities, these students would attend their traditional neighborhood school. Because the lottery did not guarantee all students in the urban district a magnet school

---

[41] The parties negotiated an agreement, which was adopted by the court as an order, and has been amended and extended over the years.

slot, a student also had to designate four other school options.[42] However, without a similar infusion of funds that was available for the magnet schools, officials we spoke to said that the neighborhood schools in the urban district declined. As a result, families that did not gain access to well-supported magnet schools resented resources spent on these schools, according to officials. Also, because the neighborhood schools were not required to maintain a specified percentage of minority students like the magnets, they, as well as the charter schools in the urban district, continued not to be very diverse, according to officials.

The state also enabled students from the urban district to enroll in traditional schools (non-magnet) in the suburbs by drawing four attendance zones around the urban district. Creation of these zones reduced bus travel times for students and facilitated relationships between parents in the community whose children were attending the same suburban school, according to officials.[43] Parents could apply for these traditional, suburban schools through the lottery, selecting up to five participating suburban school districts that are designated within their zone. If a student was not placed in one of these schools, they would attend a school in their urban district. In addition to providing transportation so that students could attend suburban schools, the state offered suburban schools grants of up to $8,000 per student, an academic and social support grant of up to $115,000 per school district, and a capital funds grant of up to $750,000 per school district. Despite these incentives, according to officials we interviewed, some families chose not to enroll their children in the suburban schools and instead opted to stay in close-by neighborhood schools, dampening the effects of the efforts to diversify.

School District in the South. The district in the South had previously been under a federal desegregation order and experienced major demographic changes going from a district serving primarily Black and White students

---

[42] There are two separate lotteries—(1) one for urban district residents to attend a school within the district and (2) one for residents and non-residents to attend a school outside the district. All urban district residents can apply through a lottery to attend a school in the urban district or a separate lottery to attend a (1) magnet school or (2) an open choice (non-magnet) school outside the urban district. Non-residents who wish to attend a magnet school or an open choice school must apply through that lottery.

[43] This effort also allowed suburban and rural students to attend schools in a nearby urban center.

to one serving many other races and ethnicities as well as immigrant populations.[44] Students in the district represented about 120 different nationalities and languages, and according to officials, this included students from Somalia and Coptic Christians and Kurds from Egypt. To address the major demographic changes and help achieve diversity across more schools in the district, the district did away with its previous school attendance zones, which had generally assigned students to schools located in their geographic area or neighborhood.[45] In its place, the district created new student assignment zones for its schools, and also hired an outside expert to help implement a new diversity plan. Specifically, under the new student assignment plan, the new zones were intended to provide greater socioeconomic and racial diversity nearer to where students lived, according to school district officials we interviewed. Under the new plan, parents were allowed to choose among schools within their attendance zones, which allow greater choice of schools for children closer to their neighborhoods. The plan also supported students who chose to attend schools outside of these zones by providing public transit passes, while school bus transportation was provided to students who attended schools within their attendance zones.

According to documents we reviewed, this district experienced challenges implementing its revised student assignment plan. Parents' choices of schools resulted in resegregation of students, prompting a complaint leading to a Department of Education investigation, as well as a federal lawsuit. According to Education officials, their investigation of the complaint found that after the school choice period was completed and students were enrolled for the school year, there was a significant increase in racial isolation in some of the schools in particular urban and

---

[44] The school district achieved "unitary" status in 1998.

[45] Before the district created new student assignment zones, the district had 12 attendance areas called clusters, each defined by the attendance area of a single high school. Each cluster also included two or more middle schools and at least several elementary schools. Generally, students residing within the geographic area that comprised a single cluster were zoned into a school within that cluster. However, students living in some residential areas were zoned into "noncontiguous" areas outside the cluster in which they resided.

suburban areas.[46] In addition, several families and a nonprofit organization filed a federal lawsuit alleging that the implementation of the school district's revised student assignment plan was causing unconstitutional racial segregation in the district.[47] The court upheld the plan, finding that although the plan had caused a "segregative effect" in the district, there was no discriminatory intent by the officials in adopting and implementing the plan.[48] To address the concerns raised in the lawsuit, the district hired an expert to refine and develop a school diversity plan. Under this diversity plan, student diversity was defined broadly, to include language and disability, as well as race/ethnicity and income (see text box). However, even after implementing the new diversity plan, officials told us that some families in their district sent their children to private schools, rather than attend the district's public schools. These officials also said that, in their opinion, some White families in their district were less eager to have their children attend diverse schools.

Diversity Plan in a School District in the South

According to district documents, a school in the district is "diverse" if it meets

at least one of the following measures:

- enrolls multiple racial/ethnic groups, and no single group represents more than 50 percent of the school's total enrollment;
- enrolls at least three racial/ethnic groups, and each represents at least 15 percent of the school's total enrollment; or
- enrolls at least two racial/ethnic groups, and each represents at least 30 percent of the school's total enrollment; and

at least two of the following measures:

- percentage of students eligible for free or reduced meals is at least two-thirds the average of other schools,
- percentage of English Learners is at least two-thirds the average of other schools, or
- percentage of students with a disability is at least two-thirds the average of other schools.

The district measures schools within their grade tier level. The typical grade tier levels are

---

[46] The complaint, filed with Education's Office for Civil Rights in 2009, alleged that the school district's student assignment plan was causing racial resegregation in the district. In 2015, the district entered into a resolution agreement with Education, in which the district agreed to implement certain actions, including providing supplemental resources, enhancing communication with parents, and conducting additional reporting.

[47] This lawsuit was filed in 2009.

[48] The court then determined that the plan was rationally related to legitimate government interests and therefore passed constitutional muster. This 2012 decision was later affirmed on appeal.

elementary school (Pre-K–4th grade), middle school (5th-8th grade), and high school (9th-12th grade).

Source: Diversity plan of selected school district in the South. | GAO-16-345

As part of the new diversity plan, the district is also hiring staff that reflect, to the extent possible, the diversity of the student body.[49] Further, when making decisions about a range of matters, such as drawing school boundary lines, placement of new schools, providing student transportation, and recruiting and training school staff, the plan calls for them to consider the impact of those decisions on diversity. In addition, the district is in the process of allocating school resources with a goal of better reflecting the different needs of students in the schools (e.g., English Learners).[50]

School District in the West. The district we visited in the West is located in a state with an "open-enrollment" law, which gives parents a significant degree of choice in determining the schools their children attend, including schools outside of their neighborhoods. District officials told us that, in their opinion, as a result of the state law, White students often choose not to attend certain schools in the district. District officials told us that this left a largely Hispanic and low-income student population in those schools, prompting the district to implement several actions in an attempt to diversify. Specifically, the district, led by the school board, converted some of its existing public schools into magnet schools. Further, to meet diverse student needs, the state provided additional funds for high-needs students, such as those eligible for free or reduced-price lunch, English Learners, or foster care youth.[51]

According to officials, this district struggled to diversify because parents have a significant degree of choice in where to enroll their children,

---

[49] As part of the new diversity plan, the district also measures racial/ethnic diversity of school staff who are certified and non-certified, comparing the diversity of these staff to the average of other schools.

[50] The district is adopting student-based budgeting, which uses a funding formula with "weights" for specific student characteristics. Schools are given additional funding above the base amount per student based on student characteristics, such as English Learners, students with disabilities, low income students, and students with low academic performance.

[51] In this state, according to officials, schools are primarily supported by state funds, but local funds may also be available to supplement district and school budgets.

magnet schools give priority to children in their neighborhood, and funding was limited for some schools. After the district implemented its diversity efforts, district officials told us that, in their opinion, some White families continued to choose schools outside the district and many other families chose to keep their children in neighborhood schools where diversity was low. In addition, the magnet schools gave priority to neighborhood children, which further hampered attempts at diversity. Further, although the district converted some of its schools to magnet schools to attract students, they provided no transportation for students, and some of the schools were converted without any upgrades to the facilities, as state funding for education declined due to an economic recession. One principal we interviewed at a converted magnet school expressed frustration that his school did not have the proper signage or visual appeal to attract families. Further, principals and other school district officials we interviewed said that they struggled to reach capacity in some of their schools. In contrast, one of the magnet schools we visited had a waiting list and was a state-of-the-art facility, with Wi-Fi, computers for every student, and 3D printers. Unlike the other magnet schools, this school has been operating as a magnet for nearly 20 years, and at the time of our review, had a waiting list. In further contrast, this school received most of its funding from private donations at a level significant enough to fund the technology focus of this school.

Education and Justice Have Taken a Range of Actions to Address Racial Discrimination against Students, although Better Use of Available Data May Enhance These Efforts

Education Addresses Discrimination by Conducting Investigations, Issuing Guidance, and Providing Technical Assistance

Education has taken a range of actions to address racial discrimination in schools.[52] For example, Education has conducted investigations on its own initiative as well as investigations in response to complaints or reports of possible discrimination. Depending on the outcome of these investigations, Education may enter into agreements, called resolution agreements, which establish the actions a school or school district agrees to take to address issues found during an investigation. Education also may withhold federal funds if a recipient is in violation of the civil rights laws and Education is unable to reach agreement with the parties, although officials told us that this rarely happens.[53]

Education's agency-initiated investigations, which are called compliance reviews, target problems that appear particularly acute. Education's Office for Civil Rights launched 32 compliance reviews in fiscal years 2013 and 2014 across a range of issues related to racial discrimination. For example, in 2014 Education completed a compliance review of an entire district's disciplinary practices. As a result of that review, Education found that Black students were disproportionately represented among students

---

[52] As previously mentioned, Education is responsible for enforcing a number of civil rights laws, which protect students from discrimination on the basis of other traits, like sex and disability. This report focuses on Education's efforts to prevent and address discrimination on the basis of race, color, or national origin.

[53] For Education's regulations implementing Title VI of the Civil Rights Act of 1964, see 34 C.F.R. pt. 100. Before withholding of federal funds can occur, a recipient, among other things, has the right to request a hearing.

subject to suspensions, other disciplinary actions, and referrals to law enforcement and that Black students were disciplined differently from White students for similar offenses. In one instance, Education cited an example of an 8th-grade White student who was given detention for leaving class without permission while an 8th-grade Black student was suspended 3 days for skipping a class even though this student had no such prior incidents. Education entered into a resolution agreement with the district to resolve the issues it identified, which, among other things, required the district to collect data to monitor its disciplinary practices for potential discrimination. The agreement also required the district to assign a staff person responsible for ensuring that disciplinary practices are equitable and to provide training for teachers and staff.[54] In 2013, another compliance review initiated by Education of a district found that Black and Hispanic students were under-represented in high school honors and AP courses, as well as elementary and middle school advanced courses and gifted and talented programs. To resolve these issues, Education entered into a resolution agreement with the district which, among other things, required the district to identify potential barriers to student participation in these courses, such as eligibility and selection criteria, hire a consultant to help address this issue, and provide training for district and school staff on how to encourage and retain student participation in these courses. The agreement also required the district to collect and evaluate data on an ongoing annual basis of its enrollment policies, practices, and procedures to determine whether they are being implemented in a non-discriminatory manner.

Further, Education has also conducted more narrowly-focused investigations in response to complaints of discrimination, which can be filed by anyone who believes that an educational institution that receives federal funds has discriminated against someone on the basis of race, color, or national origin. According to Education, it received about 2,400 such complaints in fiscal year 2014. For example, in response to a 2011 complaint alleging that a high school's football coach subjected Black players to racial harassment and that the district failed to address it, Education launched an investigation of the district. Education found that the football coach directed racial slurs at Black players, and players who complained were harassed by their fellow students and staff, who

---

[54] A list of recent compliance reviews and complaint resolutions can be found on Education's Office for Civil Rights' website at http://www2.ed.gov/about/offices/list/ocr/frontpage/faq/readingroom.html.

supported the coach. Education also found that the coach did not assist Black players with obtaining athletic scholarships, even stating that athletic scholarships are for White players and financial aid is for Black players. To resolve these findings, Education negotiated a resolution agreement with the district that required the district to review and revise its harassment and discrimination policies and take appropriate steps to remedy the harassment by the coach, including appointing a new coach and offering counseling for the students.

Education has also issued guidance to schools on their obligations under the federal civil rights laws, and its decision to issue such guidance may be prompted by factors such as its findings from investigations or developments in case law. For example, Education issued guidance jointly with Justice in 2014 on school discipline to assist states, districts, and schools in developing practices and strategies to enhance the atmosphere in the school and ensure those policies and practices comply with federal law.[55] The guidance included a letter on applicable federal civil rights laws and discipline that describes how schools can meet their obligations under federal law to administer student discipline without discriminating against students on the basis of race, color, or national origin. Also in that year, Education issued guidance addressing the issue of equitable access to educational resources.[56] Specifically, in its guidance, Education states that chronic and widespread racial disparities in access to rigorous courses, academic programs, and extracurricular activities and in other areas "hinder the education of students of color today" and strongly recommends that school districts proactively assess their policies and practices to ensure that students are receiving educational resources without regard to their race, color, or national origin. In addition, Education issued guidance jointly with Justice in 2011 following the 2007 U.S. Supreme Court decision in *Parents Involved* that

---

[55] For guidance on discipline, see
http://www2.ed.gov/about/offices/list/ocr/letters/colleague-201401-title-vi.pdf.

[56] For guidance on resource equity, see
http://www2.ed.gov/about/offices/list/ocr/letters/colleague-resourcecomp-201410.pdf.

addressed districts' voluntary use of race to diversify their schools.[57] This guidance sets forth examples of the types of actions school districts could take to diversify their schools or avoid racial isolation, consistent with this decision and the federal civil rights laws. It states that districts should first consider approaches that do not rely on the race of individual students, for example, by using race-neutral criteria such as students' socioeconomic status, before adopting approaches that rely on individual racial classifications. For approaches that do consider a students' race as a factor, districts should ensure their approach closely fits their goals and considers race only as one factor among other non-racial considerations. Further, Education also offers technical assistance, through various means, such as conducting webinars, sponsoring and presenting at conferences, and disseminating resource guides to schools and school districts. For example, at a 2015 magnet school workshop, Education officials discussed the benefits to improving diversity in the schools and the ramifications of relevant court decisions related to diversifying schools. They also offered examples of actions schools can take consistent with these court decisions to promote greater school diversity.

Analyses of Civil Rights Data by School Groupings Could Help Education Discern Further Disparities

Education uses its Civil Rights Data to identify patterns, trends, disparities, and potential discrimination by performing analysis of particular groups of students, such as by race and ethnicity, and could further enhance its current efforts by also more routinely analyzing data by school types and groupings. Analyzing data by schools may help discern patterns and trends occurring in different types of schools, such as the disparities our analysis revealed in high-poverty schools comprised

---

[57] As discussed previously, in 2007, in *Parents Involved in Community Schools v. Seattle School District No. 1*, the Court struck down several school districts' student assignment plans that relied on racial classification. 551 U.S. 701 (2007). For the guidance on the use of race to achieve diversity, see http://www2.ed.gov/about/offices/list/ocr/docs/guidance-ese-201111.pdf. Also, Education issued additional guidance in both 2013 and 2014 that reaffirmed the continued viability of this 2011 guidance on the voluntary use of race, following recent U.S. Supreme Court decisions concerning race in the context of education or the political process, and the agency has cited the guidance in its notices for competitive grants. For this additional guidance, see http://www.ed.gov/ocr/letters/colleague-201309.pdf (2013), http://www.ed.gov/ocr/docs/dcl-qa-201309.pdf (2013), and http://www.ed.gov.ocr/letters/colleague-201405-schuette-guidance.pdf (2014).

of mostly Black or Hispanic students.[58] For example, through its analysis of its Civil Rights Data, Education identified an issue nationwide with disproportionately high suspension and expulsion rates of certain groups of students by race, among other characteristics.[59] Education uses these analyses to inform its investigations and guidance. For example, its analysis of its Civil Rights Data, which showed disparities across groups of students by race and other factors in students' access to academic courses (such as algebra and AP courses), helped inform an investigation and resulted in guidance.[60] According to Education, it typically analyzes its data by student groups to help it identify disparities or potential discrimination against students on the basis of race, color, or national origin, consistent with the civil rights laws it enforces.

While these analyses, by specific groups of students, are important to its enforcement responsibilities, by also more routinely analyzing data by different types and groupings of schools, other patterns might be revealed, as our own analyses show. In addition, although socioeconomic status is not a protected class under the U.S. Constitution or federal civil rights laws, research has shown that poverty (socioeconomic status) and race overlap (see app. III). By examining these two phenomena in tandem, Education has another lens for examining any possible issues at the school level. Education has used its Civil Rights Data to publish a 2014 "data snapshot" on school discipline that highlighted disparities by race, ethnicity, and English Learner status, among other characteristics. To illustrate where Education might enhance such an analysis, our analysis of the same data also found disparities and differences between groups of schools—with disparities most evident for H/PBH schools. Further, Education's data snapshot on college and career readiness, also

---

[58] Our analyses examined schools based on both their socioeconomic and racial composition. There is no legal requirement that Education do the type of analysis that we did for this report.

[59] Education's analysis also showed disparities in suspension rates by gender and disability status and expulsion rates by gender; however, for the purposes of this report, we did not include these characteristics in our analysis. See Education's data report on school discipline at http://www2.ed.gov/about/offices/list/ocr/docs/crdc-discipline-snapshot.pdf.

[60] Education's analysis of access to academic courses also showed disparities by disability status; however, for the purposes of this report, we did not include these characteristics in our analysis. See Education's data report on College and Career Readiness at http://www2.ed.gov/about/offices/list/ocr/docs/crdc-college-and-career-readiness-snapshot.pdf.

based on its analysis of Civil Rights Data, showed disparities in access to core subjects, such as algebra I and II, geometry, biology, chemistry, and AP courses by various student groups. Again, analyzing the same data, we also found these disparities, but we found them among schools grouped by level of poverty and among Black and Hispanic students, with disparities most acute among H/PBH schools. In addition, our analyses showed further disparities when we grouped schools by types— traditional, charter, and magnet schools. For example, one of our analyses of Education's school year 2011-12 data showed that, among H/PBH schools, a higher percentage of magnet schools (83 percent) offered AP courses than did the traditional schools (50 percent) or charter schools (32 percent). While Education's analyses of its Civil Rights Data provide critical information to aid its enforcement of civil rights laws, also analyzing these data by different groupings and types of schools could provide Education with an additional layer of information that, as we found, further illuminates disparities and could enhance their efforts.[61] Federal internal control standards state that agencies should use operational data to ensure effective and efficient use of agency resources.[62] By analyzing its data by groupings and types of schools, Education has an opportunity to enhance its efforts and better inform guidance and technical assistance to the groups and types of schools that need it most.

[61] In addition to Civil Rights Data, Education also has access to the Common Core of Data (CCD), which is Education's primary database for basic information and descriptive statistics for K-12 public schools. The CCD annual survey collects information about the full universe of these schools and provides general descriptive statistics on schools and school districts, students and staff data, and fiscal data.

[62] See GAO, *Internal Control Standards: Internal Control Management and Evaluation Tool*, GAO-01-1008G (Washington, D.C.: August 2001).

Justice Addresses Discrimination by Conducting Investigations, Issuing Guidance, and Taking Legal Action

The Department of Justice's Educational Opportunities Section of the Civil Rights Division has taken several actions to address racial discrimination against students.[63] Similar to Education, Justice conducts investigations in response to complaints or reports of possible violations. Depending on the outcome of its investigation and the circumstances of the case, Justice may take a number of actions, which could include entering into a settlement agreement with the district or initiating litigation to enforce the civil rights laws. For example, Justice investigated complaints in 2011 alleging that a student had been subject to racial harassment at a high school, which included receiving race-based death threats and retaliation for reporting the harassment. The investigation found that the district failed to adequately investigate, address, and prevent recurrence of the harassment, which resulted in the student leaving the district out of fear for her safety, and that other Black students had experienced racial harassment and retaliation. Justice entered into a settlement agreement with the district that included making revisions to the policies and procedures for handling racial harassment complaints.[64] Justice has also intervened, that is joined in and became a party, in discrimination lawsuits. For example, in 2000 Justice intervened in a civil rights lawsuit against a district, alleging the district failed to appropriately address harassment of a pair of students by other students. The alleged harassment included racial slurs, including some within earshot of teachers, and racial graffiti on walls and desks. Further, one of the students was the victim of a racially motivated assault. The parties negotiated an agreement, which was adopted by the court as an order, that required the district to, among other things, maintain written records of each harassment allegation received, investigation conducted, and corrective action taken by the district to ensure a consistent and effective review of allegations. Further, as previously mentioned, Justice has issued guidance jointly with Education to ensure states and school districts understand their responsibilities to prevent and address racial discrimination in schools.

---

[63] As previously mentioned, Justice is responsible for enforcing a number of civil rights laws, which protect students from discrimination on the basis of other traits, like sex, religion, and disability. This report focuses only on Justice's efforts to prevent and address discrimination on the basis of race, color and national origin.

[64] A list of some of the complaints investigated and cases brought by Justice can be found on its website at http://www.justice.gov/crt/educational-opportunities-cases, accessed 2/9/15.

Justice also monitors and enforces open federal school desegregation cases where Justice is a party to the litigation. According to Justice officials, as of November 2015 there were 178 of these cases.[65] Justice officials told us they routinely work with districts (and other parties to the desegregation case) to close out those cases where the school district has met its statutory and Constitutional duty to desegregate. For example, in January 2015, Justice completed its compliance monitoring visits for a school district that had been operating under a series of consent orders since 1970, most recently one from 2012.[66] Justice determined that the district had complied with the terms of the desegregation order. The parties agreed, and in May 2015 the court declared the district unitary, thus allowing the desegregation order to be lifted. Justice has also recently engaged in active litigation in several open desegregation cases. For example, in 2011, as a party to another long-standing desegregation case, Justice filed a motion asking the court to find that the district had violated its obligations under several prior desegregation orders. In 2012, the court determined, among other things, that although the district had made significant progress, two predominantly Black schools had never been desegregated, and the court ordered the district to draft a plan to improve integration at those schools.[67] Justice officials said that they initiate action on an open desegregation case in response to various factors, including requirements from the court, complaints or inquiries they receive, or issues raised in media reports. According to Justice officials, the agency also conducts agency-initiated "affirmative reviews" of districts under open desegregation orders, which could include requests for additional supplemental data, site visits, and initiation of negotiations if compliance issues are identified, among other things.

---

[65] Justice is not a party in all of the cases in which a court has ordered a district to desegregate. As a consequence, the 178 cases cited above do not include all of the open desegregation orders—only those to which Justice is a party to the case.

[66] The 2012 desegregation order required the school district to, among other things, adopt a random assignment process for assigning students to classrooms at one elementary school; allow intra-district transfers of students between elementary schools only in certain cases; and submit periodic reports to Justice and the court, such as classroom rosters. Under the order, the district was required to grant student transfers between elementary schools within the district only when the requested transfer satisfied the requirements of a majority-to-minority transfer or in the event of an exceptional hardship.

[67] Litigation is continuing on the desegregation plan.

Justice Does Not Systematically Track Key Data to Inform Actions on Open Desegregation Cases

As noted above, Justice is responsible for monitoring and enforcing the 178 open federal desegregation orders to which it is a party—many of which originated 30 or 40 years ago. However, it does not systematically track important summary information on these orders. As a consequence, the potential exists that some cases could unintentionally languish for long periods of time. For example, in a 2014 opinion in a long-standing desegregation case, the court described a long period of dormancy in the case and stated that lack of activity had taken its toll, noting, among other things, that the district had not submitted the annual reports required under the consent order to the court for the past 20 years. Although the court found certain disparities in educational programs and student test results, based on the record at the time it was unable to determine when the disparities arose or whether they were a result of discrimination. The court noted that had Justice "been keeping an eye" on relevant information, such as disparities in test scores, it could have brought it to the court's attention more quickly, allowing the court and district to address the issue in a timely fashion. While Justice officials told us that they maintain a system to track certain identifying information about each case, which includes the case name, the court docket number, the identification number generated by Justice, and the jurisdiction where the case originated, officials were unable to provide more detailed summary information across all of the open cases, such as the date of the last action, or the nature of the last action taken. Justice officials said that to obtain such information they would have to review each individual case file, some of which are voluminous and many of which are not stored electronically. Thus, Justice officials were unable to respond with specificity as to when or the nature of the last action taken on the open orders within broad time frames of 5 years, 10 years, or 20 years ago.

According to Justice's Strategic Plan, the agency has a goal to protect the rights of the American people and enforce federal law.[68] This Plan includes an objective for implementing this goal—to promote and protect American civil rights by preventing and prosecuting discriminatory practices. According to this Plan, Justice seeks to address and prevent discrimination and segregation in elementary and secondary schools. The Plan states that the extent to which societal attitudes and practices reflect a continuing commitment to tolerance, diversity, and equality affect the

---

[68] See United States Department of Justice, Office of the Attorney General, *Strategic Plan, Fiscal Years 2014-2018*.

scope and nature of Justice's work. In addition, federal internal control standards state that routine monitoring should be a part of normal operations to allow an agency to assess how the entity being monitored is performing over time.[69] These standards also state that agencies should use information to help identify specific actions that need to be taken and to allow for effective monitoring of activities. Specifically, the standards state that information should be available on a timely basis to allow effective monitoring of events and activities and to allow prompt reaction. Also, the standards state that information should be summarized and presented appropriately and provide pertinent information while permitting a closer inspection of details as needed. In addition, the standards state that agencies should obtain any relevant external information that may affect achievement of missions, goals, and objectives.

Without a systematic way to track key information about all of the open desegregation cases, such as the date of the last action or receipt of required reports, Justice may lack the summary information needed to monitor the status of its orders. This may affect the agency's ability to effectively manage its caseload and to promote and protect civil rights.

Conclusions

More than 60 years after the *Brown* decision, our work shows that disparities in education persist and are particularly acute among schools with the highest concentrations of minority and poor students. Further, Black and Hispanic students are increasingly attending high-poverty schools where they face multiple disparities, including less access to academic offerings. Research has shown a clear link between a school's poverty level and student academic outcomes, with higher poverty associated with worse educational outcomes. While the districts we contacted in different areas across the nation have efforts under way to help improve the quality of education for students, the Departments of Education and Justice have roles that are critical because they are responsible for enforcing federal laws that protect students from racial discrimination and ensuring schools and districts provide all students with equitable access. In doing so, both agencies can better leverage data available to them to aid their guidance, enforcement, and oversight efforts. Education has ongoing efforts to collect data that it uses to identify

---

[69] See GAO, *Internal Control Standards: Internal Control Management and Evaluation Tool*, GAO-01-1008G (Washington, D.C.: August 2001).

potential discrimination and disparities across key groups of students, but it has not routinely analyzed its data in a way that may reveal larger patterns among different types and groups of schools. As a result, the agency may miss key patterns and trends among schools that could enhance its efforts. In addition, Justice is a party to 178 federal desegregation orders that remain open, but Justice does not track key summary information about the orders that would allow them to effectively monitor their status. Without systematically tracking such information, the agency may lack information that could help in its enforcement efforts.

Recommendations for Executive Action

- We recommend that the Secretary of Education direct Education's Office for Civil Rights to more routinely analyze its Civil Rights Data Collection by school groupings and types of schools across key elements to further explore and understand issues and patterns of disparities. For example, Education could use this more detailed information to help identify issues and patterns among school types and groups in conjunction with its analyses of student groups.

- We recommend that the Attorney General of the United States direct the Department of Justice's Civil Rights Division to systematically track key summary information across its portfolio of open desegregation cases and use this data to inform its monitoring of these cases. Such information could include, for example, dates significant actions were taken or reports received.

Agency Comments and Our Evaluation

We provided a draft of this report to the Departments of Education and Justice for their review and comment. Education's written comments are reproduced in appendix IV, and Justice's written comments are reproduced in appendix V. Education also provided technical comments, which we incorporated into the report, as appropriate.

In its written comments, Education stated that its Office for Civil Rights already analyzes its Civil Rights Data Collection (Civil Rights Data) in some of the ways we recommend, and in light of our recommendation, it will consider whether additional analysis could augment the Office for Civil Rights' core civil rights enforcement mission. Specifically, Education said it is planning to conduct some of the analysis suggested in our recommendation for future published data analysis based on the 2013-2014 Civil Rights Data and will consider whether additional analysis would be helpful. Education also stated it is committed to using every tool at its disposal to ensure all students have access to an excellent education. In addition, Education stated that when appropriate, the Office for Civil Rights often uses the types of analyses recommended by GAO in its investigations. It also noted that racial disparities are only one potential element for investigations of potential discrimination. Education also said that it publishes reports based on the Civil Rights Data, referring to the Office for Civil Rights' published data snapshots on College and Career Readiness and Teacher Equity, which we reviewed as part of this study. We found they do provide some important information about schools with high and low levels of minority populations. Further, Education stated that the disaggregations of the data that we presented in our report were the type of specialized analysis that the Office for Civil Rights encourages users outside the agency to explore.

While we recognize the important ways Education is currently using its data and the additional analyses it is considering and planning in the future, it was our intent in making the recommendation that Education more routinely examine the data for any disparities and patterns across a key set of data elements by the school groupings we recommended. Further, while we support the engagement of researchers and other interested stakeholders outside the agency, we also believe that Education should conduct these analyses as part of its mission to provide oversight. We believe that by doing so, Education will be better positioned to more fully understand and discern the nature of disparities and patterns among schools.

In light of Education's response about its data analysis efforts, which we agree are consistent with good practices to use agency resources effectively and efficiently, we modified the recommendation and report accordingly. We now specify in the recommendation that Education should "more routinely" analyze its Civil Rights Data across key elements in the ways recommended by our report to help it identify disparities among schools. We believe that such analysis will enhance current efforts by identifying and addressing disparities among groups and types of schools—helping, ultimately, to improve Education's ability to target oversight and technical assistance to the schools that need it most.

In its written comments, Justice stated it believes its procedures for tracking case-related data are adequate. Nevertheless, consistent with our recommendation, Justice said it is currently developing an electronic document management system that may allow more case-related information to be stored in electronic format. Justice agreed that tracking information concerning its litigation docket is important and useful and that it shares our goal of ensuring it accurately and adequately tracks case-related information. However, Justice also stated that our report fails to appreciate the extensive amount of data the agency maintains on its desegregation cases, which it maintains primarily for the purpose of litigation. Justice stated that it tracks and preserves information received from school districts and all case-related correspondence and pleadings, and because the data it collects are used to litigate each individual case, it does not track such data across cases. We understand Justice's need to maintain voluminous case-specific evidentiary files, some of which are maintained in hard copy. It was out of recognition for the extensive nature of these files that we recommended Justice also have a way to track key, summary information across its cases. Such summary information would allow for timely and effective monitoring and for prompt reaction, in accordance with federal standards for internal control. Further, Justice said various terms in our recommendation, such as "systematically" or "key" were not clear or well defined. In deference to the agency's expertise, in making the recommendation, we intentionally used broad language that would allow Justice to make its own judgments about what would best serve its mission.

Justice also said it is concerned that the report could be read to suggest that racial disparities within a public school district constitute *per se* evidence of racial discrimination. Although our report does not make this statement, we have added additional language to further clarify that data on disparities alone are not sufficient to establish unlawful discrimination.

With respect to the report's description of a selected desegregation case, Justice stated it was concerned with the emphasis we placed on one comment in the lengthy court opinion ("…if Justice had 'been keeping an eye' on relevant information…"), which it said was based solely on the absence of entries on the court's docket sheet. Justice said in this case and in many others, it is engaged in a range of related activities, such as site visits and settlement agreements, which are not recorded on the courts' docket sheets. We appreciate that courts may not be aware of all of Justice's activities in any one case; however, we believe this case illustrates how important it is for Justice to have timely information about its cases and how better information tracking could help the agency better manage and oversee its caseload. Also, with respect to this case, Justice commented that the existence of disparities in test scores alone is not sufficient to trigger a remedy under Justice's legal authority, and Justice must consider multiple factors before taking action in a case. We have clarified in the report that data on disparities taken alone are insufficient to establish unlawful discrimination. While we understand that tracking such information may not necessarily trigger action by Justice in any particular case, the case described was selected to serve as an example of the potential benefits of more proactive tracking of information in these cases.

Further, Justice said it was concerned the report could be read to suggest that some cases have remained dormant or languished for long periods of time as a result of Justice's tracking system, without sufficient appreciation for the responsibilities of the school districts and courts in advancing and resolving the cases (such as by achieving unitary status). In the draft report on which Justice commented, we stated that the onus is on the district, not Justice, to seek unitary status. We have amended the final report to state this more prominently. However, while we acknowledge the key roles of the districts and the courts in resolving and advancing a desegregation case, the focus of our report is on the federal role, and Justice, too, plays an important role in litigating these cases—a role we believe would be enhanced by improving its tracking of information about the cases.

As agreed with your offices, unless you publicly announce the contents of this report earlier, we plan no further distribution until 30 days from the report date. At that time, we will send copies of this report to the appropriate congressional committees, the Secretary of Education and the Attorney General, and other interested parties. In addition, the report will be available at no charge on GAO's website at http://www.gao.gov.

If you or your staff have any questions about this report, please contact me at (617) 788-0580 or nowickij@gao.gov. Contact points for our Offices of Congressional Relations and Public Affairs may be found on the last page of this report. GAO staff who made key contributions to this report are listed in appendix VI.

Jacqueline M. Nowicki,
Director, Education, Workforce,
   and Income Security Issues

Appendix I: Scope and Methodology

The objectives of this study were to examine: (1) how the percentage of schools with high percentages of poor and Black or Hispanic students has changed over time and the characteristics of these schools, (2) why and how selected school districts have implemented actions to increase student diversity, and (3) the extent to which the Departments of Education (Education) and Justice (Justice) have taken actions to identify and address issues related to racial discrimination in schools.

Analysis of Federal Datasets

Population Focus and Definitions

To answer our objectives, we analyzed the (1) poverty level of schools and (2) Black and Hispanic student composition of schools, as a basis for grouping and comparing schools.[1] We measured poverty level at the school level using the percentage of students eligible for free or reduced-price lunch. A student is generally eligible for free or reduced-price lunch based on federal income eligibility guidelines that are tied to the federal poverty level and the size of the family.[2] We focused on Black and Hispanic students because they are the two largest minority groups in U.S. K-12 public schools, and existing research has suggested that these groups experience disparities in school. The thresholds and measure of poverty discussed here and below was commonly used in the literature and also aligns with how Education analyzes its data.

---

[1] For information presented in the text, figures, and tables, we computed all calculations based on Education's data.

[2] Education's National Center for Education Statistics uses eligibility for free or reduced-price lunch as a measure of poverty. The Department of Agriculture's National School Lunch Program provides low-cost or free lunches to children in schools. Children are eligible for free lunches if their household income is below 130 percent of federal poverty guidelines or if they meet certain automatic eligibility criteria, such as eligibility for the Supplemental Nutrition Assistance Program or Temporary Assistance for Needy Families. Students are eligible for reduced-price lunches if their household income is between 130 percent and 185 percent of federal poverty guidelines. For example, the maximum household income for a family of four to qualify for free lunch benefits was $30,615 in school year 2013-2014. Recent changes in the school lunch program may result in changes in how schools implement the program and how they report counts of students who are eligible for free or reduced-price lunch to Education. These changes could affect data analysis using free or reduced-price lunch eligibility as a proxy for poverty. We do not have evidence these changes substantively affected our analysis. See, for example, Department of Education, *Free and Reduced-Price Lunch Eligibility Data in EDFacts: A White Paper on Current Status and Potential Changes* (2012).

We categorized schools for our analysis based on both the percent of students in a school eligible for free or reduced-price lunch _and_ the percent of Black or Hispanic students collectively in a school (see table 1). We divided our data into three school groups as follows:

1. Schools whose student populations were comprised of 0 to 25 percent students eligible for free or reduced-price lunch (i.e., low-poverty) _and_ 0 to 25 percent Black or Hispanic students (referred to as "L/PBH schools"),

2. Schools whose student populations were comprised of 75 to 100 percent students eligible for free or reduced-price lunch (i.e., high-poverty) _and_ 75 to 100 percent Black or Hispanic students (referred to as "H/PBH schools"), and

3. Schools that fall outside of these two categories (referred to as "all other schools").

Because the literature also suggests that schools with even higher levels of Blacks and Hispanics and poverty face disparities that are even more acute, we also analyzed the group of schools in which 90 to 100 percent of the students were eligible for free or reduced-price lunch and 90 to 100 percent of the students were Black or Hispanic. These schools represent 6 percent of all K-12 public schools and are included in appendix II for further comparison. Our analyses of Education's data in this report are intended to describe selected characteristics of these schools; they should not be used to make conclusions about the presence or absence of unlawful discrimination.

Table 1: Percentage and Number of U.S. K-12 Public Schools by Poverty Levels and Levels of Black or Hispanic Students, School Year 2013-14

	Schools with 0 to 25 percent Black or Hispanic students	Schools with 26 to 74 percent Black or Hispanic students	Schools with 75 to 100 percent Black or Hispanic students
Schools with 0 to 25 percent students eligible for free or reduced-price lunch	16 percent 14,508 schools (L/PBH schools)	2 percent 2,258 schools	1 percent 473 schools
Schools with 26 to 74 percent students eligible for free or reduced-price lunch	31 percent 28,930 schools	20 percent 18,901 schools	4 percent 3,626 schools
Schools with 75 to 100 percent students eligible for free or reduced-price lunch	3 percent 2,825 schools	7 percent 6,848 schools	16 percent 15,089 schools (H/PBH schools)

Source: GAO analysis of Department of Education, Common Core of Data, 2013-14. | GAO-16-345

Notes: Throughout this report, we use the term "all other schools" to refer to schools that are shown in this table above that are not labelled L/PBH or H/PBH schools. This table excludes schools that did not report information on (1) free or reduced-price school lunch, which we used as a proxy to categorize the poverty level of the school or (2) the number of Black or Hispanic students, which we used to categorize the level of Black or Hispanic students in the school. Percentages do not add to 100 percent due to rounding.

Analysis of the Common Core of Data

To describe how the percentage and characteristics of schools with different levels of poverty among students and Black or Hispanic students has changed over time, we analyzed schools with both the highest and lowest percentages of poverty and Blacks or Hispanics and schools with all other percentages of these groups (see table 1). We used Education's Common Core of Data (CCD) from school years 2000-01, 2005-06, 2010-11, and 2013-14, the most recent year of data available for these analyses. CCD is administered by Education's National Center for Education Statistics, which annually collects non-fiscal data about all public schools, as well as fiscal and non-fiscal data on public school districts, and state education agencies in the United States. The data are supplied by state education agency officials describing their schools and school districts. Data elements include name, address, and phone number of the school or school district; demographic information about students and staff; and fiscal data, such as revenues and current expenditures. To assess the reliability of these data, we reviewed technical documentation and interviewed relevant officials from Education. Based on these efforts, we determined that these data were sufficiently reliable for our purposes. The data in the CCD represent the full universe of all U.S. K-12 public schools.[3] To further understand the trends underlying the growth or decline of these categories of schools, we examined whether any variation in growth existed by region (Northeastern, Midwestern, Southern, and Western areas of the United States) and school type (traditional neighborhood schools, charter schools, and magnet schools). For our analysis of the CCD, we excluded schools that did not report information on (1) free or reduced-price lunch, which we used as a proxy to categorize the poverty level of the school or (2) the number of Black or Hispanic students, which we used to categorize the level of Black or Hispanic students in the school. For school year 2000-01, we included 78,194 schools and excluded 16,520 schools; for school year 2005-06, we included 91,910 schools and

---

[3] CCD refers to K-12 public schools as "elementary and secondary schools". In addition, the CCD collected data on pre-K students; for school year 2013-14, there were about 1.1 million pre-K students (2 percent of all students) and about 309,000 pre-K students in H/PBH schools (4 percent of all students in H/PBH schools).

excluded 8,717 schools; for school year 2010-11, we included 94,612 schools and excluded 7,413 schools; and for school year 2013-14, we included 93,458 schools and excluded 7,633 schools. Because CCD collects information on the universe of schools, these exclusions would not affect our overall findings.

There are several sources of non-sampling error associated with the CCD, which is self-reported and collected from the universe of schools and school districts. Non-sampling errors can be introduced in many ways. For example, they can result from data processing or data entry, when respondents misinterpret survey questions, do not follow survey instructions, or do not follow the item definitions correctly. Further, while CCD's coverage of traditional public schools and school districts is very complete, coverage of publicly funded education outside of traditional school districts has varying levels of coverage within different states and jurisdictions. Some states do not report schools that are administered by state organizations other than state educational agencies. Examples include charter schools authorized by an organization that is not a school district, schools sponsored by health and human services agencies within a state, and juvenile justice facilities. In recent years, Education has increased efforts to identify schools that may be underreported by state educational agencies. Further, because this information is self-reported, there is also the potential for misreporting of information. Education attempts to minimize these errors in several ways, including through training, extensive quality reviews, and data editing.[4]

Analysis of the Civil Rights Data Collection

To examine additional characteristics about schools the students attended, we analyzed data from the public use file of Education's Civil Rights Data Collection (referred to as the Civil Rights Data in this report) for school year 2011-12, which was the most recent year of data available. The Civil Rights Data—collected on a biennial basis—consists

---

[4] See Glander, M., *Documentation to the NCES Common Core of Data Public Elementary/Secondary School Universe Survey: School Year 2013–14 Provisional Version 1a* (NCES 2015-150), U.S. Department of Education (Washington, DC: National Center for Education Statistics, 2015), retrieved December 22, 2015 from http://nces.ed.gov/pubsearch, and Glander, M., *Documentation to the NCES Common Core of Data Local Education Agency Universe Survey: School Year 2013–14 Provisional Version 1a* (NCES 2015-147), U.S. Department of Education (Washington, DC: National Center for Education Statistics, 2015), retrieved December 22, 2015 from http://nces.ed.gov/pubsearch.

of data on the nation's public schools, including student characteristics and enrollment; educational and course offerings; disciplinary actions; and school environment, such as incidences of bullying. To assess the reliability of these data, we reviewed technical documentation, and interviewed relevant officials from Education. Based on these efforts, we determined that these data were sufficiently reliable for our purposes. The Civil Rights Data is part of Education's Office for Civil Rights' overall strategy for administering and enforcing the federal civil rights statutes for which it is responsible. While this information was collected from a sample of schools in previous years, it was collected from the full universe of all U.S. K-12 public schools in 2011-12.[5] By analyzing these data across the school categories in table 1, we were able to present data on the differences in the availability of courses offered among schools with different levels of poverty among students and Black or Hispanic students.[6] For example, we were able to analyze differences among schools with respect to school offerings, such as advanced math and science courses—as well as advanced academic programs, Advanced Placement courses, and Gifted and Talented Education programs. We were also able to examine differences in the level of disciplinary incidents—such as more than one out-of-school suspension, arrests related to school activity, and bullying—and the percentage of English Learners and students with disabilities. We also examined the numbers of full-time teachers with more than one year of experience, licensed and certified teachers, and teacher absences. The data also allowed us to analyze differences by type of school—traditional neighborhood schools, charter schools, and magnet schools (see app. II). For this analysis we matched schools in the Civil Rights Data for school year 2011-12 (the most year recent for which Civil Rights Data are available) to schools in the CCD for school year 2011-12 and excluded schools for which there was not a match. Further, from the Civil Rights Data, we also excluded schools that did not report (1) free or reduced-price school lunch, which we used as a proxy to categorize the poverty level of the school or (2) the

---

[5] The last time the Civil Rights Data was collected from a universe of schools and school districts was in 2000. The 2002, 2004, 2006, and 2009-10 Civil Rights Data collected data from a sample of school districts. For the 2013-14 school year, Education again collected data on all K-12 public schools in the United States, and Education anticipates that data will be publicly available in June 2016.

[6] Education's Office for Civil Rights uses the free or reduced-price lunch data collected by Education's National Center for Education Statistics and makes these data available on its Civil Rights Data website.

number of Black or Hispanic students, which we used to categorize the level of Black or Hispanic students in the school. As a result, our analysis of the Civil Rights Data for school year 2011-12 included 95,635 schools and excluded 5,675 schools. In the report, we present different years for the Civil Rights Data and CCD and, as a result, the numbers and percentages of schools and students derived from these two sets of data will not match.

As with the CCD, the school year 2011-12 Civil Rights Data collected the full universe of schools and districts, with 99.2 and 98.4 percent response rate, respectively. These data are also subject to non-sampling error, and because these data are self-reported, there is also the potential for misreporting of information. For these data, Education put in place quality control and editing procedures to reduce errors. Further, for the school year 2011-12 Civil Rights Data, respondents were to answer each question on the Civil Rights Data survey prior to certification. Null or missing data prevented a school district from completing their Civil Rights Data submission to Education's Office for Civil Rights. Therefore, in cases where a school district may not have complete data, some schools or districts may have reported a zero value in place of a null value. It is not possible to determine all possible situations where this may have occurred. As such, it may be the case that the item response rates may be positively biased. Further, within this dataset there are outliers that likely represented misreported values. These outliers had the potential to heavily influence state or national totals. To ensure the integrity of the state and national totals, the Office for Civil Rights suppressed outliers identified by data quality rules. These rules flagged inconsistent and implausible values for suppression. To mitigate the potential for suppressions that distort aggregate totals, suppressed data were replaced with imputed data where possible. For example, where the number of students disciplined exceeded the number in membership, the number was set to the number of students in membership.[7]

---

[7] For additional technical notes regarding these data, see State and National Estimation Data Notes at http://ocrdata.ed.gov/Downloads/Data%20Notes%20CRDC%202011-12%202.9.pdf.

School District Site Visits

We selected a school district in each of three states (one in the Northeast, South, and West) and interviewed officials to describe why and how selected school districts have taken actions to address the diversity of their schools. We selected states to include different regions of the country, and we selected school districts within these states that had taken action to increase diversity. Within these districts, the schools we visited were selected to include a mix of grade level (elementary, middle, and high school), school type (traditional public and magnet), and location (urban and suburban). To select districts, we relied on recommendations from subject matter specialists and a review of available information. For example, we reviewed the school districts that had participated in Education's Voluntary Public School Choice grant program.[8] Information from the districts we contacted is illustrative and not meant to reflect the situation in other districts with similar efforts.

In the districts we selected, we interviewed different stakeholders, such as school district superintendents, school board members, state education officials, community leaders, and school officials. We conducted these interviews in person (in two locations) or by phone. During our interviews, we collected information about issues related to racial and socioeconomic diversity in public schools, including types of actions implemented to increase diversity, reasons for implementing the actions, challenges faced in implementing the actions, and comments about federal actions in this area. In addition to interviewing officials, in some locations we toured schools to learn more about how and why various actions were implemented at those schools. We provided the relevant sections of a draft of this report to the appropriate officials from each district for their review. We did not assess the extent to which the selected districts have achieved any diversity goals or complied with any applicable court orders. Because we selected the school districts

---

[8] Education's Voluntary Public School Choice grant program supports efforts to establish or expand intradistrict, interdistrict, and open enrollment public school choice programs to provide parents, particularly parents whose children attend low-performing public schools, with expanded education options. Programs and projects assisted are required to use a portion of the grant funds to provide the students selected to participate in the program with transportation services, or the cost of transportation, to and from the public elementary schools and secondary schools, including charter schools, which the students choose to attend under the program. A grantee may not use funds for school construction. No more than 5 percent of the funds made available through the grant for any fiscal year may be used for administrative expenses. 20 U.S.C. §§ 7225-7225g. The Every Student Succeeds Act, enacted in December 2015, eliminated the authority for this grant program. Pub. L. No. 114-95, 129 Stat. 1802 (2015).

judgmentally, we cannot generalize the findings about the actions officials took to address diversity to all school districts and schools nationwide.

Review of Federal Actions to Address School Diversity

To assess the actions taken by the Departments of Education and Justice to address issues related to racial discrimination in schools, we interviewed agency officials and reviewed relevant federal laws, regulations, and agency documents. With both agencies, we interviewed officials about each agency's responsibilities with respect to federal civil rights laws and regulations, as well as the actions the agencies took to enforce them. With Education officials, we discussed the agency's investigations, guidance, and data collection, and we reviewed agency procedures, selected documents from recently concluded investigations, and guidance documents. With Justice officials, we discussed the agency's litigation activities, investigations, and guidance and reviewed agency procedures and guidance documents, as well as certain documents from selected court cases, including selected desegregation orders. We assessed agencies' actions using guidance on internal controls in the federal government related to oversight and monitoring as well as agency guidance and strategic plans.

We also interviewed representatives of civil rights organizations and academic experts to discuss issues related to racial and socioeconomic diversity in public schools, including actions taken by school districts to increase diversity and federal actions to enforce federal civil rights laws with respect to race in public schools.

Research on Student Outcomes

We identified studies about the effect that the racial and socioeconomic composition of K-12 public schools has on various student outcomes, using specific terms to search several bibliographic databases. From these searches, we used studies published between 2004 and 2014 on U.S. students, as these studies are more reflective of current students and their outcomes.[9] We looked at studies concerned primarily with the effect of socioeconomic composition of schools, or racial composition of schools, or both factors together. The studies selected were based on nationally representative samples of students that allowed us to examine the socioeconomic or racial composition of the schools, and the studies analyzed the effect these school-level characteristics had on student

---

[9] One of the studies included in our review was a meta-analysis that examined studies on U.S. students and also included studies on students from other countries.

academic outcomes, such as test scores, grade point average, high school graduation or dropout rates, and/or college enrollment using research methodologies that controlled for potentially confounding factors. We excluded from consideration some studies based on factors including outdated data, limited scope, or research methods that failed to control for multiple factors when assessing outcomes. Although the findings of the studies we identified are not representative of the findings of all studies looking at whether a school's racial or socioeconomic composition affects student outcomes, they provide examples of published and peer-reviewed research that used strong research designs to assess these effects. See appendix III for the list of studies we reviewed.

We conducted this performance audit from November 2014 through April 2016 in accordance with generally accepted government auditing standards. Those standards require that we plan and perform the audit to obtain sufficient, appropriate evidence to provide a reasonable basis for our findings and conclusions based on our audit objectives. We believe that the evidence obtained provides a reasonable basis for our findings and conclusions based on our audit objectives.

Appendix II: Additional Analyses of Schools with Different Levels of Poverty and Black or Hispanic Students and Their Students, Using Common Core of Data and the Civil Rights Data Collection

This appendix contains the results of our additional analyses to examine trends and disparities among schools with different levels of poverty among students and Black or Hispanic students. For these analyses, we used school- and student-level data from both the Common Core of Data (CCD) for selected school years from 2000-01 to 2013-14 and the Civil Rights Data Collection (Civil Rights Data) for school year 2011-12. This information is presented as a supplement to the findings presented in this report; however, we noted in the report when the information in these tables helped inform our findings.

Additional Analyses of Schools and Students Using CCD

These tables present the results of our additional analyses that used school- and student-level data from the Common Core of Data for students attending K-12 public schools. The tables include data on schools by different poverty levels and different concentrations of Black or Hispanic students, and data on students who attend these schools.[1] For both schools and students, we present additional data by school type (traditional, charter, and magnet schools) and by region of country.

All K-12 Students

Table 2: All Students Attending K-12 Public Schools, by Race, in Selected School Years from 2000-01 to 2013-14

Student Race	School Year 2000-01		School Year 2005-06		School Year 2010-11		School Year 2013-14	
	Number of Students	Percent of Students	Number of Students	Percent of Students	Number of Students	Percent of Students	Number of Students	Percent of Students
Black	7,861,280	17	8,372,338	17	7,853,189	16	7,743,490	16
Hispanic	7,652,131	16	9,642,142	20	11,342,335	23	12,363,690	25
White	28,160,352	60	27,754,527	57	25,768,751	52	25,002,339	50
Asian	1,925,436	4	2,242,958	5	2,446,175	5	2,576,542	5
Other	592,292	1	644,538	1	1,759,638	4	2,016,609	4
Total	46,191,491	100	48,656,503	100	49,170,088	100	49,702,670	100

Source: GAO analysis of Department of Education, Common Core of Data, school years 2000-01 to 2013-14. | GAO-16-345

[1] Table 2 shows all students who attended K-12 public schools. All other tables and figures in this report exclude schools (and their students) that did not report information on (1) free or reduced-price school lunch, which we used as a proxy to categorize the poverty level of the school or (2) the number of Black or Hispanic students, which we used to categorize the level of Black or Hispanic students in the school, unless otherwise noted.

Appendix II: Additional Analyses of Schools
with Different Levels of Poverty and Black or
Hispanic Students and Their Students, Using
Common Core of Data and the Civil Rights
Data Collection

Notes: The "Other" category includes Native Hawaiian/Other Pacific Islander, American Indian/Alaska Native, or Two or More Races. This table includes all students attending K-12 public schools. Percentages were rounded to the nearest whole number. Percentages may not add to 100 due to rounding.

Students in High-Poverty Schools Only

Figure 11: Students Attending High-Poverty Schools, by Race, School Year 2013-14

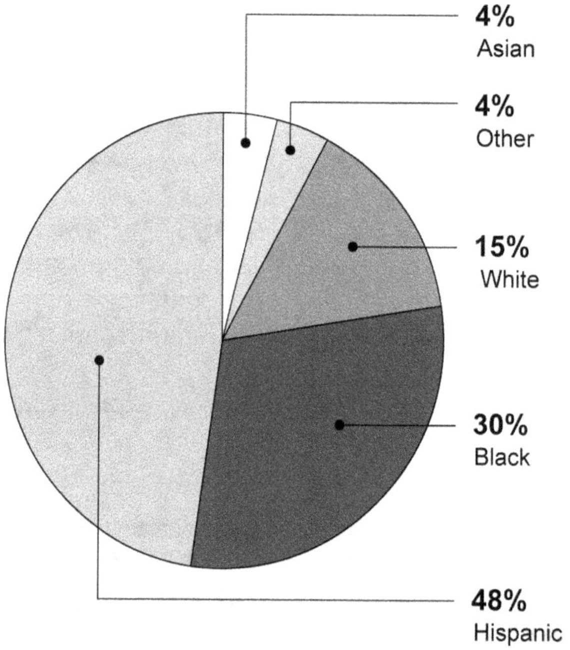

4%
Asian

4%
Other

15%
White

30%
Black

48%
Hispanic

Source: GAO analysis of Department of Education, Common Core of Data, 2013-14. | GAO-16-345

Notes: "High-poverty" refers to schools in which 75-100 percent of students were eligible for free or reduced-price lunch. The "Other" category includes Native Hawaiian/Other Pacific Islander, American Indian/Alaska Native, or Two or More Races. This figure excludes schools (and their students) that did not report information on (1) free or reduced-price school lunch, which we used as a proxy to categorize the poverty level of the school or (2) the number of Black or Hispanic students in the school. Percentages were rounded to the nearest whole number. Percentages may not add to 100 due to rounding.

Appendix II: Additional Analyses of Schools
with Different Levels of Poverty and Black or
Hispanic Students and Their Students, Using
Common Core of Data and the Civil Rights
Data Collection

Distribution of Black and Hispanic Students within Schools with High Levels of Poverty and Black or Hispanic Students

Table 3: Schools with High Levels of Poverty and Black or Hispanic Students: Number and Percent That Are Mostly Black Only, Mostly Hispanic Only, and a Mixture of Both Races, in Selected School Years from 2000-01 to 2013-14

Level of Poverty and Black or Hispanic Students in School	School Year 2000-2001		School Year 2005-2006		School Year 2010-2011		School Year 2013-2014	
	Number of schools	Percent of Schools	Number of Schools	Percent of Schools	Number of schools	Percent of Schools	Number of schools	Percent of Schools
High-poverty and mostly Black schools (75 to 100 percent Black students)	3,121	45	4,006	39	4,331	34	4,298	28
High-poverty and mostly Hispanic schools (75 to 100 percent Hispanic students)	2,082	30	3,274	32	4,263	34	5,965	40
High-poverty and mixture of Black or Hispanic schools (singularly, neither race represents 75 to 100 percent of the students, but combined they represent 75 to 100 percent of the students)	1,806	26	2,931	29	4,055	32	4,826	32
The following data are a subset of schools above and are included in the total below.								
90 to100 percent poverty and 90 to 100 percent Black schools	*1,039*	*43*	*1,317*	*38*	*1,610*	*37*	*1,800*	*31*
90 to100 percent poverty and 90 to 100 percent Hispanic schools	*556*	*23*	*844*	*25*	*1,084*	*25*	*1,798*	*30*
90 to100 percent poverty and mixture of Black or Hispanic schools (singularly, neither race represents 90 to 100 percent of the students, but combined they represent 90 to 100 percent of the students)	*832*	*34*	*1,263*	*37*	*1,662*	*38*	*2,300*	*39*
Total	7,009	100	10,211	100	12,649	100	15,089	100

Source: GAO analysis of Department of Education, Common Core Data, school years 2000-01 to 2013-14. | GAO-16-345

Notes: High-poverty schools are defined as schools in which 75 to 100 percent of students were eligible for free or reduced-price lunch. This table excludes schools that did not report information on (1) free or reduced-price school lunch, which we used as a proxy to categorize the poverty level of the school or (2) the number of Black or Hispanic students, which we used to categorize the level of

Appendix II: Additional Analyses of Schools
with Different Levels of Poverty and Black or
Hispanic Students and Their Students, Using
Common Core of Data and the Civil Rights
Data Collection

Black or Hispanic students in the school. Percentages were rounded to the nearest whole number. Percentages may not add to 100 due to rounding.

Students in Schools by Different Levels of Poverty, by Race

Table 4: Students Attending Schools with Different Levels of Poverty, by Race, in Selected School Years from 2000-01 to 2013-14

Level of poverty in schools		School Year 2000-01		School Year 2005-06		School Year 2010-11		School Year 2013-14	
		Number of Students	Percent of Students by Racial Category	Number of Students	Percent of Students by Racial Category	Number of Students	Percent of Students by Racial Category	Number of Students	Percent of Students by Racial Category
Low-poverty schools	Black	1,101,643	15	1,043,476	13	644,806	8	512,623	7
	Hispanic	1,081,091	16	1,473,488	15	1,431,405	13	942,396	8
	White	13,109,031	53	12,389,119	45	8,444,571	33	7,301,646	30
	Asian	752,746	43	974,116	44	900,303	37	900,589	35
	Other	97,869	22	97,315	17	349,233	20	376,883	19
All other schools	Black	3,786,525	53	4,426,192	54	3,900,524	50	3,515,104	46
	Hispanic	3,378,478	49	4,672,520	49	5,542,798	49	5,433,037	44
	White	10,985,880	44	13,942,423	51	15,632,999	61	15,494,255	63
	Asian	753,552	43	965,189	43	1,171,652	48	1,208,675	47
	Other	250,931	56	329,749	58	1,005,909	57	1,176,526	59
High-poverty schools	Black	2,262,714	32	2,788,685	34	3,261,055	42	3,658,245	48
	Hispanic	2,373,788	35	3,418,154	36	4,322,164	38	5,919,731	48
	White	868,701	3	1,133,010	4	1,603,428	6	1,893,285	8
	Asian	230,097	13	288,200	13	364,206	15	451,882	18
	Other	100,492	22	140,697	25	400,124	23	443,105	22
Total	**Black**	7,150,882	100	8,258,353	100	7,806,385	100	7,685,972	100
	Hispanic	6,833,357	100	9,564,162	100	11,296,367	100	12,295,164	100
	White	24,963,612	100	27,464,552	100	25,680,998	100	24,689,186	100
	Asian	1,736,395	100	2,227,505	100	2,436,161	100	2,561,146	100
	Other	449,292	100	567,761	100	1,755,266	100	1,996,514	100

Source: GAO analysis of Department of Education, Common Core Data, school years 2000-01 to 2013-14. | GAO-16-345

Notes: Low-poverty schools are defined as schools in which 0 to 25 percent of students were eligible for free or reduced-price lunch. High-poverty schools are defined as schools in which 75 to 100 percent of students were eligible for free or reduced-price lunch. "All other schools" refers to schools that fall outside of the two categories of schools. The "Other" category includes Native Hawaiian/Other Pacific Islander, American Indian/Alaska Native, and Two or More Races. This table excludes schools (and their students) that did not report information on (1) free or reduced-price school lunch, which we used as a proxy to categorize the poverty level of the school or (2) the

Appendix II: Additional Analyses of Schools
with Different Levels of Poverty and Black or
Hispanic Students and Their Students, Using
Common Core of Data and the Civil Rights
Data Collection

number of Black or Hispanic students in the school. Percentages were rounded to the nearest whole number. Percentages may not add to 100 due to rounding.

Schools and Students by Different Levels of Poverty and by Black or Hispanic Students

Table 5: Schools with Different Levels of Poverty and Black or Hispanic Students, in Selected School Years from 2000-01 to 2013-14

Level of Poverty and Black or Hispanic Students in School	School Year 2000-01		School Year 2005-06		School Year 2010-11		School Year 2013-14	
	Number of Schools	Percent of Schools	Number of Schools	Percent of Schools	Number of Schools	Percent of Schools	Number of Schools	Percent of Schools
Low-poverty and 0 to 25 percent Black or Hispanic schools (L/PBH)	23,878	31	22,772	25	16,627	18	14,508	16
All other schools	47,307	60	58,927	64	65,336	69	63, 861	68
High-poverty and 75 to 100 percent Black or Hispanic schools (H/PBH)	7,009	9	10,211	11	12,649	13	15,089	16
The following data are a subset of H/PBH schools and are included in the total below								
90 to100 percent poverty and 90 to 100 percent Black or Hispanic schools	*2,427*	*3*	*3,424*	*4*	*4,356*	*5*	*5,898*	*6*
Total	78,194	100	91,910	100	94,612	100	93,458	100

Source: GAO analysis of Department of Education, Common Core of Data, school years 2000-01 to 2013-14. | GAO-16-345

Notes: Low-poverty schools are defined as schools in which 0 to 25 percent of students were eligible for free or reduced-price lunch. High-poverty schools are defined as schools in which 75 to 100 percent of students were eligible for free or reduced-price lunch. "All other schools" refers to schools that fall outside of the two categories of L/PBH schools and H/PBH schools. This table excludes schools that did not report information on (1) free or reduced-price school lunch, which we used as a proxy to categorize the poverty level of the school or (2) the number of Black or Hispanic students, which we used to categorize the level of Black or Hispanic students in the school. Percentages were rounded to the nearest whole number. Percentages may not add to 100 due to rounding.

Appendix II: Additional Analyses of Schools
with Different Levels of Poverty and Black or
Hispanic Students and Their Students, Using
Common Core of Data and the Civil Rights
Data Collection

Table 6: Students Attending Schools with Different Levels of Poverty and Black or Hispanic Students, in Selected School Years from 2000-01 to 2013-14

Level of Poverty and Black or Hispanic Students in School	School Year 2000-01		School Year 2005-06		School Year 2010-11		School Year 2013-14	
	Number of Students	Percent of Students	Number of Students	Percent of Students	Number of Students	Percent of Students	Number of Students	Percent of Students
Low-poverty and 0 to 25 percent Black or Hispanic schools (L/PBH)	13,529,267	33	13,182,317	27	9,542,256	19	8,523,872	17
All other schools	23,519,798	57	29,607,314	61	32,793,651	67	32,318,041	66
High-poverty and 75 to 100 percent Black or Hispanic schools (H/PBH)	4,126,783	10	5,613,663	12	6,640,946	14	8,386,069	17
The following data are a subset of H/PBH schools and are included in the total below								
90 to100 percent poverty and 90 to 100 percent Black or Hispanic schools	*1,410,218*	*3*	*1,841,227*	*4*	*2,128,159*	*4*	*3,092,895*	*6*
Total	**41,175,848**	**100**	**48,403,294**	**100**	**48,976,853**	**100**	**49,227,982**	**100**

Source: GAO analysis of Department of Education, Common Core of Data, school years 2000-01 to 2013-14. | GAO-16-345

Notes: Low-poverty schools are defined as schools in which 0 to 25 percent of students were eligible for free or reduced-price lunch. High-poverty schools are defined as schools in which 75 to 100 percent of students were eligible for free or reduced-price lunch. "All other schools" refers to schools that fall outside of the two categories of L/PBH schools and H/PBH schools. This table excludes schools (and their students) that did not report information on (1) free or reduced-price school lunch, which we used as a proxy to categorize the poverty level of the school or (2) the number of Black or Hispanic students, which we used to categorize the level of Black or Hispanic students in the school. Percentages were rounded to the nearest whole number. Percentages may not add to 100 due to rounding.

Appendix II: Additional Analyses of Schools
with Different Levels of Poverty and Black or
Hispanic Students and Their Students, Using
Common Core of Data and the Civil Rights
Data Collection

Schools and Students, by School Type

Table 7: Schools with Different Levels of Poverty and Black or Hispanic Students, by School Type, in Selected School Years from 2000-01 to 2013-14

School Type	School Year 2000-01		School Year 2005-06		School Year 2010-11		School Year 2013-14	
	Number of Schools	Percent of Schools	Number of Schools	Percent of Schools	Number of Schools	Percent of Schools	Number of Schools	Percent of Schools
Low-Poverty and 0 to 25 percent Black or Hispanic Schools (L/PBH)								
Traditional	23,395	98	21,767	96	15,556	94	13,512	93
Charter	381	2	725	3	874	5	768	5
Magnet	102	<1	280	1	197	1	228	2
Total	23,878	100	22,772	100	16,627	100	14,508	100
All Other Schools								
Traditional	45,775	97	55,330	94	60,578	93	58,505	92
Charter	788	2	1,948	3	2,879	4	3,354	5
Magnet	744	2	1,649	3	1,879	3	2,002	3
Total	47,307	100	58,927	100	65,336	100	63,861	100
High-Poverty and 75 to 100 percent Black or Hispanic Schools (H/PBH)								
Traditional	6,616	94	8,948	88	10,758	85	12,250	81
Charter	203	3	635	6	1,374	11	2,031	13
Magnet	190	3	628	6	517	4	808	5
Total	7,009	100	10,211	100	12,649	100	15,089	100

The following data are a subset of the H/PBH schools and are included in the total above

90 to 100 poverty and 90 to 100 percent Black or Hispanic Schools

School Type	Number of Schools	Percent of Schools	Number of Schools	Percent of Schools	Number of Schools	Percent of Schools	Number of Schools	Percent of Schools
Traditional	*2,323*	*96*	*3,012*	*88*	*3,698*	*85*	*4,807*	*82*
Charter	*61*	*3*	*230*	*7*	*528*	*12*	*865*	*15*
Magnet	*43*	*2*	*182*	*5*	*130*	*3*	*226*	*4*
Total	*2,427*	*100*	*3,424*	*100*	*4,356*	*100*	*5,898*	*100*

Source: GAO analysis of Department of Education, Common Core of Data, school years 2000-01 to 2013-14. | GAO-16-345

Notes: Low-poverty schools are defined as schools in which 0 to 25 percent of students were eligible for free or reduced-price lunch. High-poverty schools are defined as schools in which 75 to 100 percent of students were eligible for free or reduced-price lunch. "All other schools" refers to schools that fall outside of the two categories of L/PBH schools and H/PBH schools. The data for 90 to 100 percent poverty and 90 to 100 percent Black or Hispanic schools are a subset of the H/PBH school group. Percent refers to the percentage among a particular concentration of poor, Black or Hispanic students. For example, in school year 2000-01, among all schools that were high-poverty and had 75 to 100 percent Black or Hispanic students, 94 percent were traditional schools. This table excludes schools that did not report information on (1) free or reduced-price school lunch, which we used as a proxy to categorize the poverty level of the school or (2) the number of Black or Hispanic students, which we used to categorize the level of Black or Hispanic students in the school. Percentages were

Appendix II: Additional Analyses of Schools
with Different Levels of Poverty and Black or
Hispanic Students and Their Students, Using
Common Core of Data and the Civil Rights
Data Collection

rounded to the nearest whole number. Percentages that were less than 0.5 percent are noted as < 1 percent. Percentages may not add to 100 due to rounding.

Table 8: Students Attending Schools with Different Levels of Poverty and Black or Hispanic Students, by School Type, in Selected School Years from 2000-01 to 2013-14

School Type	School Year 2000-01		School Year 2005-06		School Year 2010-11		School Year 2013-14	
	Number of Students	Percent of Students	Number of Students	Percent of Students	Number of Students	Percent of Students	Number of Students	Percent of Students
Low-Poverty and 0 to 25 percent Black or Hispanic Schools (L/PBH)								
Traditional	13,367,548	99	12,771,782	97	9,064,773	95	7,988,037	94
Charter	90,662	1	209,251	2	319,542	3	354,465	4
Magnet	71,057	1	201,284	2	157,941	2	181,370	2
Total	**13,529,267**	**100**	**13,182,317**	**100**	**9,542,256**	**100**	**8,523,872**	**100**
All Other Schools								
Traditional	22,613,530	96	27,740,810	94	30,326,344	92	29,382,303	91
Charter	219,583	1	537,523	2	950,472	3	1,291,782	4
Magnet	686,685	3	1,328,981	4	1,516,835	5	1,643,956	5
Total	**23,519,798**	**100**	**29,607,314**	**100**	**32,793,651**	**100**	**32,318,041**	**100**
High-Poverty and 75 to 100 percent Black or Hispanic Schools (H/PBH)								
Traditional	3,918,714	95	4,927,199	88	5,845,624	88	6,922,556	83
Charter	55,477	1	178,829	3	459,345	7	795,679	9
Magnet	152,592	4	507,635	9	335,977	5	667,834	8
Total	**4,126,783**	**100**	**5,613,663**	**100**	**6,640,946**	**100**	**8,386,069**	**100**
The following data are a subset of H/PBH schools and are included in the total above								
90 to 100 percent Poverty and 90 to 100 percent Black or Hispanic Schools								
Traditional	*1,357,746*	*96*	*1,646,534*	*89*	*1,883,627*	*89*	*2,600,091*	*84*
Charter	*20,579*	*1*	*62,824*	*3*	*176,382*	*8*	*339,170*	*11*
Magnet	*31,893*	*2*	*131,869*	*7*	*68,150*	*3*	*153,634*	*5*
Total	*1,410,218*	*100*	*1,841,227*	*100*	*2,128,159*	*100*	*3,092,895*	*100*

Source: GAO analysis of Department of Education, Common Core of Data, school years 2000-01 to 2013-14. | GAO-16-345

Notes: Low-poverty schools are defined as schools in which 0 to 25 percent of students were eligible for free or reduced-price lunch. High-poverty schools are defined as schools in which 75 to 100 percent of students were eligible for free or reduced-price lunch. "All other schools" refers to schools that fall outside of the two categories of L/PBH schools and H/PBH schools. The data for 90 to 100 percent poverty and 90 to 100 percent Black or Hispanic schools are a subset of the H/PBH school group. Percent refers to the percentage among a particular concentration of poor, Black or Hispanic students. For example, in school year 2000-01, among all students who attended schools that were high-poverty and had 75 to 100 percent Black or Hispanic students, 95 percent of these students attended traditional schools. This table excludes schools (and their students) that did not report information on (1) free or reduced-price school lunch, which we used as a proxy to categorize the poverty level of the school or (2) the number of Black or Hispanic students, which we used to categorize the level of Black or Hispanic students in the school. Percentages were rounded to the nearest whole number. Percentages may not add to 100 due to rounding.

Appendix II: Additional Analyses of Schools
with Different Levels of Poverty and Black or
Hispanic Students and Their Students, Using
Common Core of Data and the Civil Rights
Data Collection

Schools and Students, by School Type and Region (Northeast, Midwest, South, West)

Table 9: Schools with Different Levels of Poverty and Black or Hispanic Students, by School Type and Region, in Selected School Years from 2000-01 to 2013-14

School Type	School Year 2000-01		School Year 2005-06		School Year 2010-11		School Year 2013-14	
	Number of Schools	Percent of Schools	Number of Schools	Percent of Schools	Number of Schools	Percent of Schools	Number of Schools	Percent of Schools
NORTHEAST								
Low-Poverty and 0 to 25 percent Black or Hispanic Schools (L/PBH)								
Traditional	6,453	99	6,334	99	5,021	99	4,408	99
Charter	35	1	57	1	42	1	61	1
Magnet	1	<1	0	0	7	<1	4	<1
Total	6,489	100	6,391	100	5,070	100	4,473	100
All Other Schools								
Traditional	5,540	98	6,526	94	7,406	95	7,460	95
Charter	105	2	178	3	234	3	268	3
Magnet	34	1	208	3	171	2	163	2
Total	5,679	100	6,912	100	7,811	100	7,891	100
High-Poverty and 75 to 100 percent Black or Hispanic Schools (H/PBH)								
Traditional	1,321	97	1,508	90	1,845	88	1,955	85
Charter	20	1	96	6	211	10	301	13
Magnet	16	1	63	4	39	2	31	1
Total	1,357	100	1,667	100	2,095	100	2,287	100
The following data are a subset of H/PBH schools and are included in the total above								
90 to 100 percent Poverty and 90 to 100 percent Black or Hispanic Schools								
Traditional	*512*	*99*	*487*	*93*	*631*	*92*	*704*	*91*
Charter	*5*	*1*	*26*	*5*	*51*	*7*	*69*	*9*
Magnet	*2*	*< 1*	*9*	*2*	*7*	*1*	*1*	*< 1*
Total	*519*	*100*	*522*	*100*	*689*	*100*	*774*	*100*

Appendix II: Additional Analyses of Schools
with Different Levels of Poverty and Black or
Hispanic Students and Their Students, Using
Common Core of Data and the Civil Rights
Data Collection

School Type	School Year 2000-01		School Year 2005-06		School Year 2010-11		School Year 2013-14	
	Number of Schools	Percent of Schools	Number of Schools	Percent of Schools	Number of Schools	Percent of Schools	Number of Schools	Percent of Schools
MIDWEST								
Low-Poverty and 0 to 25 percent Black or Hispanic Schools (L/PBH)								
Traditional	9,063	99	8,268	96	4,963	95	4,304	94
Charter	105	1	233	3	181	3	197	4
Magnet	11	<1	132	2	67	1	73	2
Total	9,179	100	8,633	100	5,211	100	4,574	100
All Other Schools								
Traditional	10,780	97	14,093	93	16,392	94	16,758	93
Charter	218	2	532	4	627	4	719	4
Magnet	113	1	481	3	497	3	504	3
Total	11,111	100	15,106	100	17,516	100	17,981	100
High-Poverty and 75 to 100 percent Black or Hispanic Schools (H/PBH)								
Traditional	599	89	1,219	75	1,522	77	1,469	72
Charter	54	8	162	10	340	17	468	23
Magnet	17	3	251	15	118	6	107	5
Total	670	100	1,632	100	1,980	100	1,954	100
The following data are a subset of H/PBH schools and are included in the total above								
90 to 100 percent Poverty and 90 to 100 percent Black or Hispanic Schools								
Traditional	*173*	*93*	*425*	*71*	*578*	*76*	*686*	*73*
Charter	*11*	*6*	*59*	*10*	*150*	*20*	*224*	*24*
Magnet	*2*	*1*	*112*	*19*	*34*	*4*	*24*	*3*
Total	*186*	*100*	*596*	*100*	*762*	*100*	*934*	*100*
SOUTH								
Low-Poverty and 0 to 25 percent Black or Hispanic Schools (L/PBH)								
Traditional	3,973	97	2,992	94	2,301	91	1,992	89
Charter	67	2	96	3	159	6	154	7
Magnet	42	1	86	3	72	3	87	4
Total	4,082	100	3,174	100	2,532	100	2,233	100
All Other Schools								
Traditional	19,656	97	21,908	95	22,805	92	21,206	92
Charter	264	1	547	2	882	4	1,008	4
Magnet	293	1	621	3	983	4	946	4
Total	20,213	100	23,076	100	24,670	100	23,160	100

Appendix II: Additional Analyses of Schools
with Different Levels of Poverty and Black or
Hispanic Students and Their Students, Using
Common Core of Data and the Civil Rights
Data Collection

School Type	School Year 2000-01		School Year 2005-06		School Year 2010-11		School Year 2013-14	
	Number of Schools	Percent of Schools	Number of Schools	Percent of Schools	Number of Schools	Percent of Schools	Number of Schools	Percent of Schools
High-Poverty and 75 to 100 percent Black or Hispanic Schools (H/PBH)								
Traditional	3,296	96	3,999	92	4,542	85	5,466	81
Charter	85	2	206	5	502	9	786	12
Magnet	67	2	146	3	290	5	474	7
Total	3,448	100	4,351	100	5,334	100	6,726	100
The following data are a subset of H/PBH schools and are included in the total above								
90 to 100 percent Poverty and 90 to 100 percent Black or Hispanic Schools								
Traditional	*1,175*	*96*	*1,409*	*93*	*1,697*	*86*	*2,445*	*81*
Charter	*27*	*2*	*75*	*5*	*199*	*10*	*389*	*13*
Magnet	*17*	*1*	*26*	*2*	*74*	*4*	*167*	*6*
Total	1,219	100	1,510	100	1,970	100	3,001	100
WEST								
Low-Poverty and 0 to 25 percent Black or Hispanic Schools (L/PBH)								
Traditional	3,906	95	4,173	91	3,271	86	2,808	8
Charter	174	4	339	7	492	13	356	11
Magnet	48	1	62	1	51	1	64	2
Total	4,128	100	4,574	100	3,814	100	3,228	100
All Other Schools								
Traditional	9,799	95	12,803	93	13,975	91	13,081	88
Charter	201	2	691	5	1,136	7	1,359	9
Magnet	304	3	339	2	228	1	389	3
Total	10,304	100	13,833	100	15,339	100	14,829	100
High-Poverty and 75 to 100 percent Black or Hispanic Schools (H/PBH)								
Traditional	1,400	91	2,222	87	2,849	88	3,360	83
Charter	44	3	171	7	321	10	476	12
Magnet	90	6	168	7	70	2	196	5
Total	1,534	100	2,561	100	3,240	100	4,032	100
The following data are a subset of H/PBH schools and are included in the total above								
90 to 100 percent Poverty and 90 to 100 percent Black or Hispanic Schools								
Traditional	*463*	*92*	*691*	*87*	*792*	*85*	*972*	*82*
Charter	*18*	*4*	*70*	*9*	*128*	*14*	*183*	*15*
Magnet	*22*	*4*	*35*	*4*	*15*	*2*	*34*	*3*
Total	*503*	*100*	*796*	*100*	*935*	*100*	*1,189*	*100*

Source: GAO analysis of Department of Education, Common Core of Data, school years 2000-01 to 2013-14. | GAO-16-345

Notes: Low-poverty schools are defined as schools in which 0 to 25 percent of students were eligible for free or reduced-price lunch. High-poverty schools are defined as schools in which 75 to 100

Appendix II: Additional Analyses of Schools
with Different Levels of Poverty and Black or
Hispanic Students and Their Students, Using
Common Core of Data and the Civil Rights
Data Collection

percent of students were eligible for free or reduced-price lunch. "All other schools" refers to schools that fall outside of the two categories of L/PBH schools and H/PBH schools. Percent refers to the percentage among a particular concentration of poor, Black or Hispanic students. For example, in school year 2000-01, of all schools in the West that were high-poverty and had 75 to 100 percent Black or Hispanic students, 91 percent were traditional schools. This table excludes schools that did not report information on (1) free or reduced-price school lunch, which we used as a proxy to categorize the poverty level of the school or (2) the number of Black or Hispanic students, which we used to categorize the level of Black or Hispanic students in the school. Percentages were rounded to the nearest whole number. Percentages that were less than 0.5 percent are noted as < 1 percent. Percentages may not add to 100 due to rounding.

Table 10: Students Attending Schools with Different Levels of Poverty and Black or Hispanic Students, by School Type and Region, in Selected School Years from 2000-01 to 2013-14

School Type	School Year 2000-01		School Year 2005-06		School Year 2010-11		School Year 2013-14	
	Number of Schools	Percent of Schools	Number of Schools	Percent of Schools	Number of Schools	Percent of Schools	Number of Schools	Percent of Schools
NORTHEAST								
Low-Poverty and 0 to 25 percent Black or Hispanic Schools (L/PBH)								
Traditional	3,715,877	100	3,731,250	99	2,932,140	99	2,510,529	99
Charter	10,063	< 1	27,215	1	12,729	< 1	28,597	1
Magnet	257	< 1	0	0	3,534	< 1	1,842	<1
Total	3,726,197	100	3,758,465	100	2,948,403	100	2,540,968	100
All Other Schools								
Traditional	2,944,392	98	3,357,773	95	3,708,340	95	3,839,575	95
Charter	29,243	1	65,010	2	103,435	3	131,293	3
Magnet	23,961	1	116,339	3	96,640	2	91,625	2
Total	2,997,596	100	3,539,122	100	3,908,415	100	4,062,493	100
High-Poverty and 75 to 100 percent Black or Hispanic Schools (H/PBH)								
Traditional	879,296	99	846,677	93	970,177	91	991,806	86
Charter	4,123	< 1	27,154	3	80,534	8	137,079	12
Magnet	8,919	1	40,053	4	21,009	2	20,282	2
Total	892,338	100	913,884	100	1,071,720	100	1,149,167	100
The following data are a subset of H/PBH schools and are included in the total above								
90 to 100 percent Poverty and 90 to 100 percent Black or Hispanic Schools								
Traditional	*333,611*	*99*	*292,294*	*96*	*319,974*	*93*	*347,257*	*93*
Charter	*996*	*< 1*	*5,988*	*2*	*21,019*	*6*	*26,040*	*7*
Magnet	*1,540*	*< 1*	*5,629*	*2*	*2,688*	*1*	*931*	*< 1*
Total	*336,147*	*100*	*303,911*	*100*	*343,681*	*100*	*374,228*	*100*

Appendix II: Additional Analyses of Schools
with Different Levels of Poverty and Black or
Hispanic Students and Their Students, Using
Common Core of Data and the Civil Rights
Data Collection

School Type	School Year 2000-01		School Year 2005-06		School Year 2010-11		School Year 2013-14	
	Number of Schools	Percent of Schools	Number of Schools	Percent of Schools	Number of Schools	Percent of Schools	Number of Schools	Percent of Schools
MIDWEST								
Low-Poverty and 0 to 25 percent Black or Hispanic Schools (L/PBH)								
Traditional	4,363,503	100	4,142,702	97	2,605,409	96	2,303,376	95
Charter	17,789	<1	48,905	1	65,548	2	81,577	3
Magnet	3,664	<1	78,229	2	43,158	2	50,628	2
Total	4,384,956	100	4,269,836	100	2,714,115	100	2,435,581	100
All Other Schools								
Traditional	3,758,085	97	5,235,277	93	6,405,305	94	6,625,189	94
Charter	56,436	1	128,650	2	145,856	2	191,077	3
Magnet	52,379	1	251,436	4	245,953	4	242,287	3
Total	3,866,900	100	5,615,363	100	6,797,114	100	7,058,553	100
High-Poverty and 75 to 100 percent Black or Hispanic Schools (H/PBH)								
Traditional	258,458	93	542,810	73	729,166	80	710,324	74
Charter	13,142	5	50,225	7	123,270	14	192,753	20
Magnet	6,157	2	154,024	21	58,429	6	56,487	6
Total	277,757	100	747,059	100	910,865	100	959,564	100
The following data are a subset of H/PBH schools and are included in the total above								
90 to 100 percent Poverty and 90 to 100 percent Black or Hispanic Schools								
Traditional	*65,918*	*95*	*187,787*	*70*	*278,265*	*80*	*336,953*	*75*
Charter	*2,662*	*4*	*15,111*	*6*	*52,826*	*15*	*95,627*	*21*
Magnet	*593*	*1*	*66,804*	*25*	*15,784*	*5*	*14,926*	*3*
Total	*69,173*	*100*	*269,702*	*100*	*346,875*	*100*	*447,506*	*100*
SOUTH								
Low-Poverty and 0 to 25 percent Black or Hispanic Schools (L/PBH)								
Traditional	2,961,972	98	2,371,023	96	1,659,057	93	1,510,572	91
Charter	14,144	<1	25,971	1	63,935	4	73,695	4
Magnet	34,324	1	83,625	3	70,564	4	77,137	5
Total	3,010,440	100	2,480,619	100	1,793,556	100	1,661,404	100
All Other Schools								
Traditional	10,811,619	98	12,498,966	94	12,964,598	91	12,299,534	90
Charter	62,810	1	153,885	1	304,943	2	412,101	3
Magnet	213,026	2	583,368	4	939,826	7	916,322	7
Total	11,087,455	100	13,236,219	100	14,209,367	100	13,627,957	100

Appendix II: Additional Analyses of Schools
with Different Levels of Poverty and Black or
Hispanic Students and Their Students, Using
Common Core of Data and the Civil Rights
Data Collection

School Type	School Year 2000-01		School Year 2005-06		School Year 2010-11		School Year 2013-14	
	Number of Schools	Percent of Schools	Number of Schools	Percent of Schools	Number of Schools	Percent of Schools	Number of Schools	Percent of Schools
High-Poverty and 75 to 100 percent Black or Hispanic Students Schools (H/PBH)								
Traditional	1,722,492	97	2,065,874	94	2,396,726	87	3,119,651	82
Charter	16,672	1	52,264	2	154,412	6	279,596	7
Magnet	30,456	2	88,836	4	197,182	7	387,354	10
Total	1,769,620	100	2,206,974	100	2,748,320	100	3,786,601	100
The following data are a subset of H/PBH schools and are included in the total above								
90 to 100 percent Poverty and 90 to 100 percent Black or Hispanic Schools								
Traditional	*582,206*	*98*	*667,664*	*95*	*807,201*	*89*	*1,314,911*	*84*
Charter	*6,588*	*1*	*20,315*	*3*	*63,985*	*7*	*146,715*	*9*
Magnet	*6,355*	*1*	*12,206*	*2*	*39,131*	*4*	*105,940*	*7*
Total	*595,149*	*100*	*700,185*	*100*	*910,317*	*100*	*1,567,566*	*100*
WEST								
Low-Poverty and 0 to 25 percent Black or Hispanic Schools (L/PBH)								
Traditional	2,326,196	97	2,526,807	95	1,868,167	90	1,663,560	88
Charter	48,666	2	107,160	4	177,330	9	170,596	9
Magnet	32,812	1	39,430	1	40,685	2	51,763	3
Total	2,407,674	100	2,673,397	100	2,086,182	100	1,885,919	100
All Other Schools								
Traditional	5,099,434	92	6,648,794	92	7,248,101	92	6,618,005	87
Charter	71,094	1	189,978	3	396,238	5	557,311	7
Magnet	397,319	7	377,838	5	234,416	3	393,722	5
Total	5,567,847	100	7,216,610	100	7,878,755	100	7,569,038	100
High-Poverty and 75 to 100 percent Black or Hispanic Schools (H/PBH)								
Traditional	1,058,468	89	1,471,838	84	1,749,555	92	2,100,775	84
Charter	21,540	2	49,186	3	101,129	5	186,251	7
Magnet	107,060	9	224,722	13	59,357	3	203,711	8
Total	1,187,068	100	1,745,746	100	1,910,041	100	2,490,737	100
The following data are a subset of H/PBH schools and are included in the total above								
90 to 100 percent Poverty and 90 to 100 percent Black or Hispanic Schools								
Traditional	*376,011*	*92*	*498,789*	*88*	*478,187*	*91*	*600,970*	*85*
Charter	*10,333*	*3*	*21,410*	*4*	*38,552*	*7*	*70,788*	*10*
Magnet	*23,405*	*6*	*47,230*	*8*	*10,547*	*2*	*31,837*	*5*
Total	*409,749*	*100*	*567,429*	*100*	*527,286*	*100*	*703,595*	*100*

Source: GAO analysis of Department of Education, Common Core of Data, school years 2000-01 to 2013-14. | GAO-16-345

Notes: Low-poverty schools are defined as schools in which 0 to 25 percent of students were eligible for free or reduced-price lunch. High-poverty schools are defined as schools in which 75 to 100

Appendix II: Additional Analyses of Schools
with Different Levels of Poverty and Black or
Hispanic Students and Their Students, Using
Common Core of Data and the Civil Rights
Data Collection

percent of students were eligible for free or reduced-price lunch. "All other schools" refers to schools that fall outside of the two categories of L/PBH schools and H/PBH schools. Percent refers to the percentage among a particular concentration of poor, Black or Hispanic students. For example, in school year 2000-01, among all students who attended schools that were high-poverty and had 75 to 100 percent Black or Hispanic students, 89 percent of these students attended traditional schools. Percentages were rounded to the nearest whole number. This table excludes schools (and their students) that did not report information on (1) free or reduced-price school lunch, which we used as a proxy to categorize the poverty level of the school or (2) the number of Black or Hispanic students, which we used to categorize the level of Black or Hispanic students in the school. Percentages were rounded to the nearest whole number. Percentages that were less than 0.5 percent are noted as < 1 percent. Percentages may not add to 100 due to rounding.

Additional Analyses of Schools and Students Using the Civil Rights Data Collection

These tables present the results of our additional analyses that used school- and student-level data from the Civil Rights Data Collection. The tables provide data on academic courses and programs offered, including advanced math and science courses and Advanced Placement and Gifted and Talented Education Programs. We also present school- and student-level data on retention and disciplinary incidents, including out-of-school suspensions, expulsions, reports of bullying, and school-related arrests, as well as data on special populations, such as English Learners and students with disabilities. We also present data on teaching-related variables, including teacher experience, certification and licensing, and absences. We present these data by different levels of poverty, Black or Hispanic students, and school type (traditional, charter, and magnet schools).

Schools That Offered or Did Not Offer Selected Academic Programs, by School Type

Table 11: Low-Poverty Schools with 0 to 25 Percent Black or Hispanic Students That Offered/Did Not Offer Course, by School Type, School Year 2011-12

School Type	Low-Poverty and 0 to 25 Percent Black or Hispanic Schools (L/PBH)				
		Course Offered		Course Not Offered	
	Total Number of Schools	Number of Schools	Percent of Schools	Number of Schools	Percent of Schools
	7th or 8th Grade Algebra				
Traditional	3,501	2,791	80	710	20
Charter	358	246	69	112	31
Magnet	50	45	90	5	10
Total	3,909	3,082	79	827	21

Appendix II: Additional Analyses of Schools
with Different Levels of Poverty and Black or
Hispanic Students and Their Students, Using
Common Core of Data and the Civil Rights
Data Collection

	Low-Poverty and 0 to 25 Percent Black or Hispanic Schools (L/PBH)				
		Course Offered		Course Not Offered	
School Type	Total Number of Schools	Number of Schools	Percent of Schools	Number of Schools	Percent of Schools
Algebra II					
Traditional	3,396	2,979	88	417	12
Charter	241	206	85	35	15
Magnet	59	58	98	1	2
Total	**3,696**	**3,243**	**88**	**453**	**12**
Geometry					
Traditional	4,113	3,798	92	315	8
Charter	311	274	88	37	12
Magnet	69	64	93	5	7
Total	**4,493**	**4,136**	**92**	**357**	**8**
Calculus					
Traditional	3,317	2,411	73	906	27
Charter	235	94	40	141	60
Magnet	58	52	90	6	10
Total	**3,610**	**2,557**	**71**	**1,053**	**29**
Biology					
Traditional	3,368	3,025	90	343	10
Charter	242	209	86	33	14
Magnet	59	58	98	1	2
Total	**3,669**	**3,292**	**90**	**377**	**10**
Chemistry					
Traditional	3,322	2,820	85	502	15
Charter	242	175	72	67	28
Magnet	58	55	95	3	5
Total	**3,622**	**3,050**	**84**	**572**	**16**
Physics					
Traditional	3,324	2,700	81	624	19
Charter	237	130	55	107	45
Magnet	58	53	91	5	9
Total	**3,619**	**2,883**	**80**	**736**	**20**
Advanced Placement Courses					
Traditional	3,260	2,419	74	841	26
Charter	234	87	37	147	63
Magnet	58	51	88	7	12

Appendix II: Additional Analyses of Schools
with Different Levels of Poverty and Black or
Hispanic Students and Their Students, Using
Common Core of Data and the Civil Rights
Data Collection

| | Low-Poverty and 0 to 25 Percent Black or Hispanic Schools (L/PBH) | | | | |
| | | Course Offered | | Course Not Offered | |
School Type	Total Number of Schools	Number of Schools	Percent of Schools	Number of Schools	Percent of Schools
Total	3,552	2,557	72	995	28
	Gifted and Talented Education Programs				
Traditional	13,583	7,565	56	6,018	44
Charter	546	188	34	358	66
Magnet	195	132	68	63	32
Total	14,324	7,885	55	6,439	45

Source: GAO analysis of Department of Education, Civil Rights Data Collection, school year 2011-12. | GAO-16-345

Notes: Low-poverty schools are defined as schools in which 0 to 25 percent of students were eligible for free or reduced-price lunch. In this table, the analysis of math and science courses is based on schools with 7th grade or higher, and includes some K-8 schools in addition to middle schools and high schools; the analysis of AP courses is based on schools with any grades between 9th and 12th grade; and the analysis of GATE programs is based on all schools. This table excludes schools that did not report whether they offered the course. For this analysis we matched schools in the Civil Rights Data to schools in the Common Core of Data and excluded schools for which there was not a match. We also excluded schools that did not report (1) free or reduced-price school lunch, which we used as a proxy to categorize the poverty level of the school and (2) the number of Black or Hispanic students, which we used to categorize the level of Black or Hispanic students in the school. Percentages were rounded to the nearest whole number. Percentages may not add to 100 due to rounding.

Table 12: All Other Schools That Offered/Did Not Offer Course, by School Type, School Year 2011-12

| | All Other Schools | | | | |
| | | Course Offered | | Course Not Offered | |
School Type	Total Number of Schools	Number of Schools	Percent of Schools	Number of Schools	Percent of Schools
	7th or 8th Grade Algebra				
Traditional	17,546	11,381	65	6,165	35
Charter	1,386	742	54	644	46
Magnet	610	522	86	88	14
Total	19,542	12,645	65	6,897	35
	Algebra II				
Traditional	15,118	12,531	83	2,587	17
Charter	1,180	935	79	245	21
Magnet	616	588	95	28	5
Total	16,914	14,054	83	2,860	17
	Geometry				
Traditional	17,078	15,126	89	1,952	11
Charter	1,272	1,089	86	183	14

Appendix II: Additional Analyses of Schools
with Different Levels of Poverty and Black or
Hispanic Students and Their Students, Using
Common Core of Data and the Civil Rights
Data Collection

School Type	Total Number of Schools	All Other Schools			
		Course Offered		Course Not Offered	
		Number of Schools	Percent of Schools	Number of Schools	Percent of Schools
Magnet	785	759	97	26	3
Total	19,135	16,974	89	2,161	11
Calculus					
Traditional	14,948	7,857	53	7,091	47
Charter	1,170	282	24	888	76
Magnet	594	449	76	145	24
Total	16,712	8,588	51	8,124	49
Biology					
Traditional	15,121	13,248	88	1,873	12
Charter	1,183	1,002	85	181	15
Magnet	600	578	96	22	4
Total	16,904	14,828	88	2,076	12
Chemistry					
Traditional	14,986	11,451	76	3,535	24
Charter	1,176	788	67	388	33
Magnet	595	558	94	37	6
Total	16,757	12,797	76	3,960	24
Physics					
Traditional	14,997	9,797	65	5,200	35
Charter	1,177	542	46	635	54
Magnet	594	508	86	86	14
Total	16,768	10,847	65	5,921	35
Advanced Placement Courses					
Traditional	14,694	7,776	53	6,918	47
Charter	1,159	338	29	821	71
Magnet	585	506	86	79	14
Total	16,438	8,620	52	7,818	48
Gifted and Talented Education Programs					
Traditional	56,411	35,953	64	20,458	36
Charter	2,540	761	30	1,779	70
Magnet	1,917	1,345	70	572	30
Total	60,868	38,059	63	22,809	37

Source: GAO analysis of Department of Education, Civil Rights Data Collection, school year 2011-12. | GAO-16-345

Notes: "All Other Schools" are defined as schools that are not (1) low-poverty schools (0 to 25
percent of students were eligible for free or reduced-price lunch) with 0 to 25 percent Black or
Hispanic students or (2) high-poverty schools (75 to 100 percent of students were eligible for free or

Appendix II: Additional Analyses of Schools
with Different Levels of Poverty and Black or
Hispanic Students and Their Students, Using
Common Core of Data and the Civil Rights
Data Collection

reduced-price lunch) with 75 to 100 percent Black or Hispanic students. In this table, the analysis of math and science courses is based on schools with 7th grade or higher, and includes some K-8 schools in addition to middle schools and high schools; the analysis of AP courses is based on schools with any grades between 9th and 12th grade; and the analysis of GATE programs is based on all schools. This table excludes schools that did not report whether they offered the course. For this analysis we matched schools in the Civil Rights Data to schools in the Common Core of Data and excluded schools for which there was not a match. We also excluded schools that did not report (1) free or reduced-price school lunch, which we used as a proxy to categorize the poverty level of the school and (2) the number of Black or Hispanic students, which we used to categorize the level of Black or Hispanic students in the school. Percentages were rounded to the nearest whole number. Percentages may not add to 100 due to rounding.

Table 13: High-Poverty Schools with 75 to 100 Percent Black or Hispanic Students That Offered/Did Not Offer Course, by School Type, School Year 2011-12

| School Type | High-Poverty and 75 to 100 Percent Black or Hispanic Schools (H/PBH) | | | | |
| | | Course Offered | | Course Not Offered | |
	Total Number of Schools	Number of Schools	Percent of Schools	Number of Schools	Percent of Schools
7th or 8th Grade Algebra					
Traditional	2,572	1,291	50	1,281	50
Charter	593	217	37	376	63
Magnet	198	150	76	48	24
Total	3,363	1,658	49	1,705	51
Algebra II					
Traditional	1,340	953	71	387	29
Charter	369	298	81	71	19
Magnet	114	110	96	4	4
Total	1,823	1,361	75	462	25
Geometry					
Traditional	1,483	1,250	84	233	16
Charter	395	347	88	48	12
Magnet	153	152	99	1	1
Total	2,031	1,749	86	282	14
Calculus					
Traditional	1,333	404	30	929	70
Charter	367	64	17	303	83
Magnet	112	65	58	47	42
Total	1,812	533	29	1,279	71
Biology					
Traditional	1,364	1,149	84	215	16
Charter	381	342	90	39	10
Magnet	115	113	98	2	2

Appendix II: Additional Analyses of Schools
with Different Levels of Poverty and Black or
Hispanic Students and Their Students, Using
Common Core of Data and the Civil Rights
Data Collection

School Type	High-Poverty and 75 to 100 Percent Black or Hispanic Schools (H/PBH)				
		Course Offered		Course Not Offered	
	Total Number of Schools	Number of Schools	Percent of Schools	Number of Schools	Percent of Schools
Total	1,860	1,604	86	256	14
Chemistry					
Traditional	1,339	947	71	392	29
Charter	368	282	77	86	23
Magnet	112	107	96	5	4
Total	1,819	1,336	73	483	27
Physics					
Traditional	1,347	725	54	622	46
Charter	370	201	54	169	46
Magnet	113	75	66	38	34
Total	1,830	1,001	55	829	45
Advanced Placement Courses					
Traditional	1,286	639	50	647	50
Charter	360	114	32	246	68
Magnet	112	93	83	19	17
Total	1,758	846	48	912	52
Gifted and Talented Education Programs					
Traditional	8,410	5,393	64	3,017	36
Charter	1,123	200	18	923	82
Magnet	556	402	72	154	28
Total	10,089	5,995	59	4,094	41

Source: GAO analysis of Department of Education, Civil Rights Data Collection, school year 2011-12. | GAO-16-345

Notes: High-poverty schools are defined as schools in which 75 to 100 percent of students were eligible for free or reduced-price lunch. In this table, the analysis of math and science courses is based on schools with 7th grade or higher, and includes some K-8 schools in addition to middle schools and high schools; the analysis of AP courses is based on schools with any grades between 9th and 12th grade; and the analysis of GATE programs is based on all schools. This table excludes schools that did not report whether they offered the course. For this analysis we matched schools in the Civil Rights Data to schools in the Common Core of Data and excluded schools for which there was not a match. We also excluded schools that did not report (1) free or reduced-price school lunch, which we used as a proxy to categorize the poverty level of the school and (2) the number of Black or Hispanic students, which we used to categorize the level of Black or Hispanic students in the school. Percentages were rounded to the nearest whole number. Percentages may not add to 100 due to rounding.

Appendix II: Additional Analyses of Schools
with Different Levels of Poverty and Black or
Hispanic Students and Their Students, Using
Common Core of Data and the Civil Rights
Data Collection

Table 14: Schools with 90 to 100 Percent Poverty and 90 to 100 Percent Black or Hispanic Students That Offered/Did Not Offer Course, by School Type, School Year 2011-12

School Type	90 to 100 Percent Poverty and 90 to 100 Percent Black or Hispanic Schools				
		Course Offered		Course Not Offered	
	Total Number of Schools	Number of Schools	Percent of Schools	Number of Schools	Percent of Schools
7th or 8th Grade Algebra					
Traditional	1,044	431	41	613	59
Charter	242	76	31	166	69
Magnet	52	36	69	16	31
Total	1,338	543	41	795	59
Algebra II					
Traditional	351	232	66	119	34
Charter	114	95	83	19	17
Magnet	15	14	93	1	7
Total	480	341	71	139	29
Geometry					
Traditional	376	309	82	67	18
Charter	126	110	87	16	13
Magnet	22	22	100	0	0
Total	524	441	84	83	16
Calculus					
Traditional	351	74	21	277	79
Charter	114	12	11	102	89
Magnet	15	5	33	10	67
Total	480	91	19	389	81
Biology					
Traditional	360	297	83	63	18
Charter	121	110	91	11	9
Magnet	16	16	100	0	0
Total	497	423	85	74	15
Chemistry					
Traditional	353	258	73	95	27
Charter	114	82	72	32	28
Magnet	15	15	100	0	0
Total	482	355	74	127	26

Appendix II: Additional Analyses of Schools
with Different Levels of Poverty and Black or
Hispanic Students and Their Students, Using
Common Core of Data and the Civil Rights
Data Collection

School Type	90 to 100 Percent Poverty and 90 to 100 Percent Black or Hispanic Schools				
	Total Number of Schools	Course Offered		Course Not Offered	
		Number of Schools	Percent of Schools	Number of Schools	Percent of Schools
Physics					
Traditional	356	193	54	163	46
Charter	115	60	52	55	48
Magnet	16	10	63	6	38
Total	487	263	54	224	46
Advanced Placement Courses					
Traditional	336	167	50	169	50
Charter	113	29	26	84	74
Magnet	15	14	93	1	7
Total	464	210	45	254	55
Gifted and Talented Education Programs					
Traditional	3,140	1,919	61	1,221	39
Charter	426	80	19	346	81
Magnet	144	105	73	39	27
Total	3,710	2,104	57	1,606	43

Source: GAO analysis of Department of Education, Civil Rights Data Collection, school year 2011-12. | GAO-16-345

Notes: The data for 90 to 100 percent schools are a subset of high-poverty and 75 to 100 percent Black or Hispanic (H/PBH) schools. In this table, the analysis of math and science courses is based on schools with 7th grade or higher, and includes some K-8 schools in addition to middle schools and high schools; the analysis of AP courses is based on schools with any grades between 9th and 12th grade; and the analysis of GATE programs is based on all schools. This table excludes schools that did not report whether they offered the course. For this analysis we matched schools in the Civil Rights Data to schools in the Common Core of Data and excluded schools for which there was not a match. We also excluded schools that did not report (1) free or reduced-price school lunch, which we used as a proxy to categorize the poverty level of the school and (2) the number of Black or Hispanic students, which we used to categorize the level of Black or Hispanic students in the school. Percentages were rounded to the nearest whole number. Percentages may not add to 100 due to rounding.

Appendix II: Additional Analyses of Schools
with Different Levels of Poverty and Black or
Hispanic Students and Their Students, Using
Common Core of Data and the Civil Rights
Data Collection

Students Attending Schools That Offered or Did Not Offer Selected Academic Programs, by School Type

Table 15: Students in Low-Poverty Schools with 0 to 25 Percent Black or Hispanic Students That Offered/Did Not Offer Course, by School Type, School Year 2011-12

School Type	Total Number of Students	Low-Poverty and 0 to 25 Percent Black or Hispanic Schools (L/PBH)					
		Course Offered				Course Not Offered	
		Number of Students in schools	Percent of Students in Schools	Number of Students Enrolled in Course	Percent of Students Enrolled in Course	Number of Students in Schools	Percent of Students in Schools
7th or 8th Grade Algebra							
Traditional	1,989,437	1,757,289	88	295,933	17	232,148	12
Charter	172,518	143,570	83	8,630	6	28,948	17
Magnet	44,066	39,728	90	6,690	17	4,338	10
Total	2,206,021	1,940,587	88	311,253	16	265,434	12
Algebra II							
Traditional	3,051,366	2,912,422	95	584,292	20	138,944	5
Charter	120,972	108,885	90	10,238	9	12,087	10
Magnet	74,831	74,716	100	16,014	21	115	<1
Total	3,247,169	3,096,023	95	610,544	20	151,146	5
Geometry							
Traditional	3,613,963	3,529,341	98	630,991	18	84,622	2
Charter	150,091	138,289	92	13,759	10	11,802	8
Magnet	83,465	82,858	99	16,001	19	607	1
Total	3,847,519	3,750,488	97	660,751	18	97,031	3
Calculus							
Traditional	2,988,144	2,598,390	87	173,385	7	389,754	13
Charter	117,767	76,608	65	2,064	3	41,159	35
Magnet	74,416	71,154	96	4,694	7	3,262	4
Total	3,180,327	2,746,152	86	180,143	7	434,175	14
Biology							
Traditional	3,019,896	2,923,385	97	778,485	27	96,511	3
Charter	120,475	113,376	94	17,868	16	7,099	6
Magnet	75,465	75,397	100	21,633	29	68	<1

Appendix II: Additional Analyses of Schools
with Different Levels of Poverty and Black or
Hispanic Students and Their Students, Using
Common Core of Data and the Civil Rights
Data Collection

School Type	Low-Poverty and 0 to 25 Percent Black or Hispanic Schools (L/PBH)						
		Course Offered				Course Not Offered	
	Total Number of Students	Number of Students in schools	Percent of Students in Schools	Number of Students Enrolled in Course	Percent of Students Enrolled in Course	Number of Students in Schools	Percent of Students in Schools
Total	3,215,836	3,112,158	97	817,986	26	103,678	3
Chemistry							
Traditional	2,988,440	2,845,820	95	602,003	21	142,620	5
Charter	120,387	102,960	86	10,458	10	17,427	14
Magnet	74,416	73,364	99	15,604	21	1,052	1
Total	3,183,243	3,022,144	95	628,065	21	161,099	5
Physics							
Traditional	2,993,178	2,823,950	94	346,283	12	169,228	6
Charter	118,210	88,916	75	5,095	6	29,294	25
Magnet	74,416	72,848	98	8,577	12	1,568	2
Total	3,185,804	2,985,714	94	359,955	12	200,090	6
Advanced Placement Courses							
Traditional	2,950,296	2,748,804	93	675,589	25	201,492	7
Charter	117,391	64,570	55	7,655	12	52,821	45
Magnet	74,416	73,065	98	21,153	29	1,351	2
Total	3,142,103	2,886,439	92	704,397	24	255,664	8
Gifted and Talented Education Programs							
Traditional	8,147,206	4,977,814	61	650,074	13	3,169,392	39
Charter	224,207	87,077	39	8,910	10	137,130	61
Magnet	153,682	110,048	72	28,984	26	43,634	28
Total	8,525,095	5,174,939	61	687,968	13	3,350,156	39

Source: GAO analysis of Department of Education, Civil Rights Data Collection, school year 2011-12. | GAO-16-345

Notes: Low-poverty schools are defined as schools in which 0 to 25 percent of students were eligible for free or reduced-price lunch. In this table, the analysis of math and science courses is based on schools with 7th grade or higher, and includes some K-8 schools in addition to middle schools and high schools; the analysis of AP courses is based on schools with any grades between 9th and 12th grade; and the analysis of GATE programs is based on all schools. This table excludes schools that did not report whether they offered the course. For this analysis we matched schools in the Civil Rights Data to schools in the Common Core of Data and excluded schools for which there was not a match. We also excluded schools that did not report (1) free or reduced-price school lunch, which we used as a proxy to categorize the poverty level of the school and (2) the number of Black or Hispanic students, which we used to categorize the level of Black or Hispanic students in the school. Percentages were rounded to the nearest whole number. Percentages may not add to 100 due to rounding.

Appendix II: Additional Analyses of Schools
with Different Levels of Poverty and Black or
Hispanic Students and Their Students, Using
Common Core of Data and the Civil Rights
Data Collection

Table 16: Students in All Other Schools That Offered/Did Not Offer Course, by School Type, School Year 2011-12

School Type	Total Number of Students	All Other Schools				Course Not Offered	
		Course Offered					
		Number of Students in Schools	Percent of Students in Schools	Number of Students Enrolled in Course	Percent of Students Enrolled in Course	Number of Students in Schools	Percent of Students in Schools
7th or 8th Grade Algebra							
Traditional	8,415,452	6,318,547	75	780,613	12	2,096,905	25
Charter	623,591	412,345	66	29,729	7	211,246	34
Magnet	457,608	401,616	88	52,887	13	55,992	12
Total	9,496,651	7,132,508	75	863,229	12	2,364,143	25
Algebra II							
Traditional	9,592,005	8,859,127	92	1,643,462	19	732,878	8
Charter	481,929	413,082	86	45,848	11	68,847	14
Magnet	793,948	779,767	98	162,127	21	14,181	2
Total	10,867,882	10,051,976	92	1,851,437	18	815,906	8
Geometry							
Traditional	11,121,993	10,618,528	95	2,002,723	19	503,465	5
Charter	527,215	460,468	87	58,905	13	66,747	13
Magnet	948,401	934,615	99	191,514	20	13,786	1
Total	12,597,609	12,013,611	95	2,253,142	19	583,998	5
Calculus							
Traditional	9,468,506	7,281,151	77	267,218	4	2,187,355	23
Charter	477,513	211,240	44	4,951	2	266,273	56
Magnet	771,505	669,174	87	28,092	4	102,331	13
Total	10,717,524	8,161,565	76	300,261	4	2,555,959	24
Biology							
Traditional	9,560,364	9,113,014	95	2,438,657	27	447,350	5
Charter	482,210	424,196	88	69,459	16	58,014	12
Magnet	776,478	767,406	99	239,286	31	9,072	1
Total	10,819,052	10,304,616	95	2,747,402	27	514,436	5
Chemistry							
Traditional	9,478,245	8,699,833	92	1,543,043	18	778,412	8
Charter	479,702	382,832	80	42,058	11	96,870	20
Magnet	772,411	757,828	98	154,649	20	14,583	2
Total	10,730,358	9,840,493	92	1,739,750	18	889,865	8

Appendix II: Additional Analyses of Schools
with Different Levels of Poverty and Black or
Hispanic Students and Their Students, Using
Common Core of Data and the Civil Rights
Data Collection

School Type	Total Number of Students	All Other Schools				Course Not Offered	
		Course Offered					
		Number of Students in Schools	Percent of Students in Schools	Number of Students Enrolled in Course	Percent of Students Enrolled in Course	Number of Students in Schools	Percent of Students in Schools
Physics							
Traditional	**9,495,268**	8,114,082	85	728,010	9	1,381,186	15
Charter	**480,010**	292,660	61	22,213	8	187,350	39
Magnet	**771,505**	727,130	94	67,411	9	44,375	6
Total	**10,746,783**	**9,133,872**	**85**	**817,634**	**9**	**1,612,911**	**15**
Advanced Placement Courses							
Traditional	**9,320,991**	7,660,672	82	1,308,603	17	1,660,319	18
Charter	**471,497**	240,104	51	27,453	11	231,393	49
Magnet	**766,611**	732,095	95	165,736	23	34,516	5
Total	**10,559,099**	**8,632,871**	**82**	**1,501,792**	**17**	**1,926,228**	**18**
Gifted and Talented Education Programs							
Traditional	**29,080,593**	20,866,249	72	1,943,120	9	8,214,344	28
Charter	**961,882**	389,191	40	30,795	8	572,691	60
Magnet	**1,552,902**	1,172,044	75	181,552	15	380,858	25
Total	**31,595,377**	**22,427,484**	**71**	**2,155,467**	**10**	**9,167,893**	**29**

Source: GAO analysis of Department of Education, Civil Rights Data Collection, school year 2011-12. | GAO-16-345

Notes: "All Other Schools" are defined as schools that are not (1) low-poverty schools (0 to 25 percent of students were eligible for free or reduced-price lunch) with 0 to 25 percent Black or Hispanic students or (2) high-poverty schools (75 to 100 percent of students were eligible for free or reduced-price lunch) with 75 to 100 percent Black or Hispanic students. In this table, the analysis of math and science courses is based on schools with 7th grade or higher, and includes some K-8 schools in addition to middle schools and high schools; the analysis of AP courses is based on schools with any grades between 9th and 12th grade; and the analysis of GATE programs is based on all schools. This table excludes schools that did not report whether they offered the course. For this analysis we matched schools in the Civil Rights Data to schools in the Common Core of Data and excluded schools for which there was not a match. We also excluded schools that did not report (1) free or reduced-price school lunch, which we used as a proxy to categorize the poverty level of the school and (2) the number of Black or Hispanic students, which we used to categorize the level of Black or Hispanic students in the school. Percentages were rounded to the nearest whole number. Percentages may not add to 100 due to rounding.

Appendix II: Additional Analyses of Schools
with Different Levels of Poverty and Black or
Hispanic Students and Their Students, Using
Common Core of Data and the Civil Rights
Data Collection

Table 17: Students in High-Poverty Schools with 75 to 100 Percent Black or Hispanic Students That Offered/Did Not Offer Course, by School Type, School Year 2011-12

School Type	Total Number of Students	High-Poverty and 75 to 100 Percent Black or Hispanic Schools (H/PBH)					
		Course Offered				Course Not Offered	
		Number of Students in Schools	Percent of Students in Schools	Number of Students Enrolled in Course	Percent of Students Enrolled in Course	Number of Students in Schools	Percent of Students in Schools
		7th or 8th Grade Algebra					
Traditional	1,363,469	797,784	59	75,608	9	565,685	41
Charter	266,360	114,815	43	9,397	8	151,545	57
Magnet	136,142	110,665	81	8,679	8	25,477	19
Total	1,765,971	1,023,264	58	93,684	9	742,707	42
		Algebra II					
Traditional	788,552	653,907	83	126,602	19	134,645	17
Charter	169,845	146,147	86	19,913	14	23,698	14
Magnet	113,573	108,494	96	22,401	21	5,079	4
Total	1,071,970	908,548	85	168,916	19	163,422	15
		Geometry					
Traditional	897,776	832,579	93	166,672	20	65,197	7
Charter	183,227	166,800	91	25,904	16	16,427	9
Magnet	147,165	146,349	99	28,162	19	816	1
Total	1,228,168	1,145,728	93	220,738	19	82,440	7
		Calculus					
Traditional	784,676	403,205	51	12,150	3	381,471	49
Charter	168,676	56,325	33	1,516	3	112,351	67
Magnet	111,423	74,865	67	2,149	3	36,558	33
Total	1,064,775	534,395	50	15,815	3	530,380	50
		Biology					
Traditional	802,904	742,875	93	203,392	27	60,029	7
Charter	173,842	162,127	93	31,263	19	11,715	7
Magnet	113,299	112,466	99	31,446	28	833	1
Total	1,090,045	1,017,468	93	266,101	26	72,577	7
		Chemistry					
Traditional	786,645	696,027	88	138,091	20	90,618	12
Charter	169,454	145,730	86	21,760	15	23,724	14
Magnet	111,423	109,386	98	19,258	18	2,037	2
Total	1,067,522	951,143	89	179,109	19	116,379	11

Appendix II: Additional Analyses of Schools
with Different Levels of Poverty and Black or
Hispanic Students and Their Students, Using
Common Core of Data and the Civil Rights
Data Collection

School Type	High-Poverty and 75 to 100 Percent Black or Hispanic Schools (H/PBH)						
		Course Offered				Course Not Offered	
	Total Number of Students	Number of Students in Schools	Percent of Students in Schools	Number of Students Enrolled in Course	Percent of Students Enrolled in Course	Number of Students in Schools	Percent of Students in Schools
Physics							
Traditional	791,405	591,679	75	75,734	13	199,726	25
Charter	170,110	111,169	65	13,241	12	58,941	35
Magnet	112,272	84,925	76	6,849	8	27,347	24
Total	1,073,787	787,773	73	95,824	12	286,014	27
Advanced Placement Courses							
Traditional	759,351	590,816	78	70,885	12	168,535	22
Charter	166,123	83,993	51	8,955	11	82,130	49
Magnet	111,423	102,009	92	14,390	14	9,414	8
Total	1,036,897	776,818	75	94,230	12	260,079	25
Gifted and Talented Education Programs							
Traditional	4,550,337	3,160,147	69	167,570	5	1,390,190	31
Charter	449,076	86,971	19	4,630	5	362,105	81
Magnet	364,283	265,999	73	17,335	7	98,284	27
Total	5,363,696	3,513,117	65	189,535	5	1,850,579	35

Source: GAO analysis of Department of Education, Civil Rights Data Collection, school year 2011-12. | GAO-16-345

Notes: High-poverty schools are defined as schools in which 75 to 100 percent of students were eligible for free or reduced-price lunch. In this table, the analysis of math and science courses is based on schools with 7th grade or higher, and includes some K-8 schools in addition to middle schools and high schools; the analysis of AP courses is based on schools with any grades between 9th and 12th grade; and the analysis of GATE programs is based on all schools. This table excludes schools that did not report whether they offered the course. For this analysis we matched schools in the Civil Rights Data to schools in the Common Core of Data and excluded schools for which there was not a match. We also excluded schools that did not report (1) free or reduced-price school lunch, which we used as a proxy to categorize the poverty level of the school and (2) the number of Black or Hispanic students, which we used to categorize the level of Black or Hispanic students in the school. Percentages were rounded to the nearest whole number. Percentages may not add to 100 due to rounding.

Appendix II: Additional Analyses of Schools
with Different Levels of Poverty and Black or
Hispanic Students and Their Students, Using
Common Core of Data and the Civil Rights
Data Collection

Table 18: Students in Schools with 90 to 100 Percent Poverty and 90 to 100 Percent Black or Hispanic Students That Offered/Did Not Offer Course, by School Type, School Year 2011-12

| | | 90 to 100 Percent Poverty and 90 to 100 Percent Black or Hispanic Schools | | | | | |
| | | Course Offered | | | | Course Not Offered | |
School Type	Total Number of Students	Number of Students in Schools	Percent of Students in Schools	Number of Students Enrolled in Course	Percent of Students Enrolled in Course	Number of Students in Schools	Percent of Students in Schools
7th or 8th Grade Algebra							
Traditional	529,347	251,322	47	21,279	8	278,025	53
Charter	106,720	32,647	31	2,829	9	74,073	69
Magnet	31,639	23,640	75	1,439	6	7,999	25
Total	667,706	307,609	46	25,547	8	360,097	54
Algebra II							
Traditional	174,255	125,580	72	24,382	19	48,675	28
Charter	50,673	44,590	88	5,396	12	6,083	12
Magnet	12,236	8,997	74	1,849	21	3,239	26
Total	237,164	179,167	76	31,627	18	57,997	24
Geometry							
Traditional	191,261	171,825	90	36,559	21	19,436	10
Charter	54,768	49,669	91	7,051	14	5,099	9
Magnet	16,866	16,866	100	2,889	17	0	0
Total	262,895	238,360	91	46,499	20	24,535	9
Calculus							
Traditional	174,255	52,879	30	1,708	3	121,376	70
Charter	50,673	4,960	10	294	6	45,713	90
Magnet	12,236	3,388	28	200	6	8,848	72
Total	237,164	61,227	26	2,202	4	175,937	74
Biology							
Traditional	179,383	160,206	89	42,069	26	19,177	11
Charter	53,093	49,036	92	8,650	18	4,057	8
Magnet	13,085	13,085	100	3,094	24	0	0
Total	245,561	222,327	91	53,813	24	23,234	9
Chemistry							
Traditional	174,866	147,581	84	28,714	19	27,285	16
Charter	50,673	41,837	83	5,686	14	8,836	17
Magnet	12,236	12,236	100	1,927	16	0	0
Total	237,775	201,654	85	36,327	18	36,121	15

Appendix II: Additional Analyses of Schools
with Different Levels of Poverty and Black or
Hispanic Students and Their Students, Using
Common Core of Data and the Civil Rights
Data Collection

	90 to 100 Percent Poverty and 90 to 100 Percent Black or Hispanic Schools						
		Course Offered				Course Not Offered	
School Type	Total Number of Students	Number of Students in Schools	Percent of Students in Schools	Number of Students Enrolled in Course	Percent of Students Enrolled in Course	Number of Students in Schools	Percent of Students in Schools
Physics							
Traditional	176,542	118,202	67	15,250	13	58,340	33
Charter	51,004	32,426	64	3,650	11	18,578	36
Magnet	13,085	8,216	63	716	9	4,869	37
Total	240,631	158,844	66	19,616	12	81,787	34
Advanced Placement Courses							
Traditional	166,248	116,102	70	14,639	13	50,146	30
Charter	49,606	22,188	45	1,803	8	27,418	55
Magnet	12,236	11,927	97	1,415	12	309	3
Total	228,090	150,217	66	17,857	12	77,873	34
Gifted and Talented Education Programs							
Traditional	1,595,868	1,029,939	65	48,185	5	565,929	35
Charter	168,995	35,111	21	1,632	5	133,884	79
Magnet	78,430	54,976	70	2,086	4	23,454	30
Total	1,843,293	1,120,026	61	51,903	5	723,267	39

Source: GAO analysis of Department of Education, Civil Rights Data Collection, school year 2011-12. | GAO-16-345

Notes: The data for 90 to 100 percent schools are a subset of high-poverty and 75 to 100 percent Black or Hispanic (H/PBH) schools. In this table, the analysis of math and science courses is based on schools with 7th grade or higher, and includes some K-8 schools in addition to middle schools and high schools; the analysis of AP courses is based on schools with any grades between 9th and 12th grade; and the analysis of GATE programs is based on all schools. This table excludes schools that did not report whether they offered the course. For this analysis we matched schools in the Civil Rights Data to schools in the Common Core of Data and excluded schools for which there was not a match. We also excluded schools that did not report (1) free or reduced-price school lunch, which we used as a proxy to categorize the poverty level of the school and (2) the number of Black or Hispanic students, which we used to categorize the level of Black or Hispanic students in the school. Percentages were rounded to the nearest whole number. Percentages may not add to 100 due to rounding.

Appendix II: Additional Analyses of Schools
with Different Levels of Poverty and Black or
Hispanic Students and Their Students, Using
Common Core of Data and the Civil Rights
Data Collection

Students Enrolled in Advanced Placement Courses, by Race

Table 19: Students Enrolled in At Least One Advanced Placement (AP) Course in Schools with Different Levels of Poverty and Black or Hispanic Students, by Race, School Year 2011-12

Student Race	Low-Poverty and 0 to 25 Percent Black or Hispanic Schools (L/PBH)			All Other Schools			High-Poverty and 75 to 100 Percent Black or Hispanic Schools (H/PBH)		
	Total Number of Students	Number of Students Enrolled in at Least One AP Course	Percent of Students Enrolled in at Least One AP Course	Total Number of Students	Number of Students Enrolled in at Least One AP Course	Percent of Students Enrolled in at Least One AP Course	Total Number of Students	Number of Students Enrolled in at Least One AP Course	Percent of Students Enrolled in at Least One AP Course
Black	123,246	18,667	15	1,394,427	158,407	11	388,522	38,963	10
Hispanic	179,963	31,078	17	1,971,053	302,906	15	326,063	44,617	14
White	2,307,711	551,802	24	4,535,314	852,542	19	37,819	5,846	15
Asian	200,006	86,433	43	421,806	136,518	32	13,905	3,308	24
Other	75,513	16,417	22	310,271	51,419	17	10,509	1,496	14
Total	2,886,439	704,397	24	8,632,871	1,501,792	17	776,818	94,230	12

The following data are a subset of H/PBH schools and are included in the total above

90 to 100 Percent Poverty and 90 to 100 Percent Black or Hispanic Schools									
Black	*79,662*	*8,226*	*10*						
Hispanic	*66,123*	*9,026*	*14*						
White	*2,176*	*294*	*14*						
Asian	*936*	*167*	*18*						
Other	*1,320*	*144*	*11*						
Total	*150,217*	*17,857*	*12*						

Source: GAO analysis of Department of Education, Civil Rights Data Collection, school year 2011-12. | GAO-16-345

Notes: Low-poverty schools are defined as schools in which 0 to 25 percent of students were eligible for free or reduced-price lunch. High-poverty schools are defined as schools in which 75 to 100 percent of students were eligible for free or reduced-price lunch. "All other schools" refers to schools that fall outside of the two categories of L/PBH schools and H/PBH schools. The "Other" category includes Native Hawaiian/Other Pacific Islander, American Indian/Alaska Native, and Two or More Races. In this table, the analysis of AP courses is based on schools with any grades between 9th and 12th grade that offered at least one AP course. For this analysis we matched schools in the Civil Rights Data to schools in the Common Core of Data and excluded schools for which there was not a match. We also excluded schools that did not report (1) free or reduced-price school lunch, which we used as a proxy to categorize the poverty level of the school and (2) the number of Black or Hispanic students, which we used to categorize the level of Black or Hispanic students in the school. Percentages were rounded to the nearest whole number.

Student Retention, Discipline, and Special Populations, by School Type

Table 20: Students Who Were Retained, Disciplined, and Were Special Populations in Schools with Different Levels of Poverty and Black or Hispanic Students, by School Type, School Year 2011-12

School Type	Low-Poverty and 0 to 25 Percent Black or Hispanic Schools (L/PBH)		All Other Schools		High-Poverty and 75 to 100 Percent Black or Hispanic Schools (H/PBH)		Row Total	Low-Poverty and 0 to 25 Percent Black or Hispanic Schools (L/PBH)		All Other Schools		High-Poverty and 75 to 100 Percent Black or Hispanic Schools (H/PBH)		Row Total
	Total Number of Students	Percent of Students	Total Number of Students	Percent of Students	Total Number of Students	Percent of Students		Number of Students	Percent of Students	Number of Students	Percent of Students	Number of Students	Percent of Students	
	Total Students							**Students Retained in 9th Grade**						
Traditional	707,142	22	2,344,570	72	209,050	6	3,260,762	13,746	7	150,070	77	32,306	16	196,122
Charter	16,710	14	68,832	59	30,251	26	115,793	1,600	12	7,838	60	3,570	27	13,008
Magnet	17,283	7	209,648	81	31,756	12	258,687	363	2	17,794	83	3,199	15	21,356
Total	741,135	20	2,623,050	72	271,057	7	3,635,242	15,709	7	175,702	76	39,075	17	230,486
	Total Students							**Students With More Than One Out-of-School Suspension**						
Traditional	8,147,206	20	29,080,593	70	4,550,337	11	41,778,136	77,058	6	931,657	74	258,278	20	1,266,993
Charter	224,758	14	964,198	59	452,026	28	1,640,982	1,668	3	27,683	47	29,203	50	58,554
Magnet	153,682	7	1,552,902	75	364,283	18	2,070,867	1,393	1	96,564	71	38,753	28	136,710
Total	8,525,646	19	31,597,693	69	5,366,646	12	45,489,985	80,119	5	1,055,904	72	326,234	22	1,462,257
	Total Students							**Students Expelled**						
Traditional	8,147,206	20	29,080,593	70	4,550,337	11	41,778,136	11,332	8	110,838	77	20,847	15	143,017
Charter	224,758	14	964,198	59	452,026	28	1,640,982	196	3	2,986	53	2,466	44	5,648
Magnet	153,682	7	1,552,902	75	364,283	18	2,070,867	245	3	5,480	67	2,444	30	8,169

GAO-16-345 Student Diversity

Appendix II: Additional Analyses of Schools with Different Levels of Poverty and Black or Hispanic Students and Their Students, Using Common Core of Data and the Civil Rights Data Collection

School Type	Low-Poverty and 0 to 25 Percent Black or Hispanic Schools (L/PBH) Total Number of Students	Percent of Students	All Other Schools Total Number of Students	Percent of Students	High-Poverty and 75 to 100 Percent Black or Hispanic Schools (H/PBH) Total Number of Students	Percent of Students	Row Total	Low-Poverty and 0 to 25 Percent Black or Hispanic Schools (L/PBH) Number of Students	Percent of Students	All Other Schools Number of Students	Percent of Students	High-Poverty and 75 to 100 Percent Black or Hispanic Schools (H/PBH) Number of Students	Percent of Students	Row Total
Total	8,525,646	19	31,597,693	69	5,366,646	12	45,489,985	11,773	8	119,304	76	25,757	16	156,834
Total Students / Students Arrested Related to School Activity														
Traditional	8,147,206	20	29,080,593	70	4,550,337	11	41,778,136	3,023	14	15,366	73	2,780	13	21,169
Charter	224,758	14	964,198	59	452,026	28	1,640,982	22	5	312	72	101	23	435
Magnet	153,682	7	1,552,902	75	364,283	18	2,070,867	10	1	727	79	180	20	917
Total	8,525,646	19	31,597,693	69	5,366,646	12	45,489,985	3,055	14	16,405	73	3,061	14	22,521
Total Students / Students with Reports of Bullying														
Traditional	8,147,206	20	29,080,593	70	4,550,337	11	41,778,136	13,646	17	59,900	75	6,337	8	79,883
Charter	224,758	14	964,198	59	452,026	28	1,640,982	152	5	1,773	56	1,221	39	3,146
Magnet	153,682	7	1,552,902	75	364,283	18	2,070,867	98	4	1,388	63	702	32	2,188
Total	8,525,646	19	31,597,693	69	5,366,646	12	45,489,985	13,896	16	63,061	74	8,260	10	85,217
Total Students / Students Who Were English Learners														
Traditional	8,147,206	20	29,080,593	70	4,550,337	11	41,778,136	209,251	6	2,500,786	67	1,043,103	28	3,753,140
Charter	224,758	14	964,198	59	452,026	28	1,640,982	3,438	2	76,826	55	59,071	42	139,335
Magnet	153,682	7	1,552,902	75	364,283	18	2,070,867	5,384	3	132,750	73	44,661	24	182,795
Total	8,525,646	19	31,597,693	69	5,366,646	12	45,489,985	218,073	5	2,710,362	67	1,146,835	28	4,075,270
Total Students / Students with Disabilities														
Traditional	8,147,206	20	29,080,593	70	4,550,337	11	41,778,136	871,779	18	3,541,003	72	533,393	11	4,946,175
Charter	224,758	14	964,198	59	452,026	28	1,640,982	19,995	13	90,662	58	44,570	29	155,227
Magnet	153,682	7	1,552,902	75	364,283	18	2,070,867	11,897	6	157,250	74	42,814	20	211,961
Total	8,525,646	19	31,597,693	69	5,366,646	12	45,489,985	903,671	17	3,788,915	71	620,777	12	5,313,363

Source: GAO analysis of Department of Education, Civil Rights Data Collection, school year 2011-12. | GAO-16-345

GAO-16-345 Student Diversity

Appendix II: Additional Analyses of Schools with Different Levels of Poverty and Black or Hispanic Students and Their Students, Using Common Core of Data and the Civil Rights Data Collection

Notes: Low-poverty schools are defined as schools in which 0 to 25 percent of students were eligible for free or reduced-price lunch. High-poverty schools are defined as schools in which 75 to 100 percent of students were eligible for free or reduced-price lunch. "All other schools" refers to schools that fall outside of the two categories of L/PBH schools and H/PBH schools. The data on "Students Retained in 9th Grade" is based on analysis of only schools with 9th grade. This table excludes schools that did not report the information across the categories in this table. For this analysis we matched schools in the Civil Rights Data to schools in the Common Core of Data and excluded schools for which there was not a match. We also excluded schools that did not report (1) free or reduced-price school lunch, which we used as a proxy to categorize the poverty level of the school and (2) the number of Black or Hispanic students, which we used to categorize the level of Black or Hispanic students in the school. Percentages were rounded to the nearest whole number. Percentages may not add to 100 due to rounding.

Appendix II: Additional Analyses of Schools
with Different Levels of Poverty and Black or
Hispanic Students and Their Students, Using
Common Core of Data and the Civil Rights
Data Collection

Table 21: Students Who Were Retained, Disciplined, and Special Populations in Schools with 90 to 100 Percent Poverty and 90 to 100 Percent Black or Hispanic Students, By School Type, School Year 2011-12

School Type	Number of Students in 90 to 100 Percent Schools	Percent of All Students
Students Retained in 9th Grade		
Traditional	6,089	3
Charter	827	6
Magnet	173	1
Total	**7,089**	**3**
Students With More Than One Out- of-School Suspension		
Traditional	81,823	6
Charter	11,733	20
Magnet	8,437	6
Total	**101,993**	**7**
Students Expelled		
Traditional	6,873	5
Charter	1,053	19
Magnet	519	6
Total	**8,445**	**5**
Students Arrested Related to School Activity		
Traditional	782	4
Charter	24	6
Magnet	47	5
Total	**853**	**4**
Students with Reports of Bullying		
Traditional	2,834	4
Charter	237	8
Magnet	196	9
Total	**3,267**	**4**
Students Who Were English Learners		
Traditional	393,112	10
Charter	29,340	21
Magnet	9,975	5
Total	**432,427**	**11**

Appendix II: Additional Analyses of Schools
with Different Levels of Poverty and Black or
Hispanic Students and Their Students, Using
Common Core of Data and the Civil Rights
Data Collection

School Type	Number of Students in 90 to 100 Percent Schools	Percent of All Students
Students with Disabilities		
Traditional	184,647	4
Charter	15,435	10
Magnet	9,621	5
Total	**209,703**	**4**

Source: GAO analysis of Department of Education, Civil Rights Data Collection, school year 2011-12. | GAO-16-345

Notes: The data for 90 to 100 percent schools are a subset of high-poverty and 75 to 100 percent Black and Hispanic (H/PBH) schools. The data on "Students Retained in 9th Grade" is based on analysis of only schools with 9th grade. This table excludes schools that did not report the information across the categories in this table. For this analysis we matched schools in the Civil Rights Data to schools in the Common Core of Data and excluded schools for which there was not a match. We also excluded schools that did not report (1) free or reduced-price school lunch, which we used as a proxy to categorize the poverty level of the school and (2) the number of Black or Hispanic students, which we used to categorize the level of Black or Hispanic students in the school. Percentages were rounded to the nearest whole number.

Teacher Experience, Certification, and Absences

Table 22: Average School-Level Estimates of Teacher Experience, Licensing/Certification, and Absences, School Year 2011-12

	Low-Poverty and 0 to 25 Percent Black or Hispanic Schools (L/PBH)	All Other Schools	High-Poverty and 75 to 100 Percent Black or Hispanic Schools (H/PBH)	*This is a subset of the H/PBH schools* *90 to 100 Percent Poverty and 90 to 100 Percent Black or Hispanic Schools*
Average Percentage of Full-Time Equivalent Teachers with More Than 1 Year Experience	96	95	92	*92*
Average Percentage of Full-Time Equivalent Teachers Meeting All State Licensing/Certification Requirements	99	98	95	*95*
Average Percentage of Full-Time Equivalent Teachers Absent More Than 10 School Days	30	32	32	*31*

Source: GAO analysis of Department of Education, Civil Rights Data Collection, school year 2011-12. | GAO-16-345

Notes: Low-poverty schools are defined as schools in which 0 to 25 percent of students were eligible for free or reduced-price lunch. High-poverty schools are defined as schools in which 75 to 100 percent of students were eligible for free or reduced-price lunch. "All Other Schools" refers to schools that fall outside of the two categories of L/PBH schools and H/PBH schools. This table excludes schools that did not report the information across the categories in this table. For this analysis we matched schools in the Civil Rights Data to schools in the Common Core of Data and excluded schools for which there was not a match. We also excluded schools that did not report (1) free or

Appendix II: Additional Analyses of Schools
with Different Levels of Poverty and Black or
Hispanic Students and Their Students, Using
Common Core of Data and the Civil Rights
Data Collection

reduced-price school lunch, which we used as a proxy to categorize the poverty level of the school and (2) the number of Black or Hispanic students, which we used to categorize the level of Black or Hispanic students in the school. Percentages were rounded to the nearest whole number.

Appendix III: List of Studies on Student Outcomes We Reviewed

The following studies examined the effects of poverty and/or racial composition of schools on student outcomes:

Aikens, Nikki L. and Oscar Barbarin. "Socioeconomic Differences in Reading Trajectories: The Contribution of Family, Neighborhood, and School Contexts." *Journal of Educational Psychology*, vol. 100, no. 2 (2008): 235-251.

Berends, Mark and Roberto Peñaloza. "Increasing Racial Isolation and Test Score Gaps in Mathematics: A 30-Year Perspective." *Teachers College Record*, vol. 112, no. 4 (2010): 978-1007.

Borman, Geoffrey D. and Maritza Dowling. "Schools and Inequality: A Multilevel Analysis of Coleman's Equality of Educational Opportunity Data." *Teachers College Record*, vol. 112, no. 5 (2010): 1201-1246.

Condron, Dennis J. "Social Class, School and Non-School Environments, and Black/White Inequalities in Children's Learning." *American Sociological Review*, vol. 74, no. 5 (2009): 683-708.

Crosnoe, Robert. "Low-Income Students and the Socioeconomic Composition of Public High Schools." *American Sociological Review*, vol. 74, no. 5 (2009): 709-730.

Goldsmith, Pat Rubio. "Schools or Neighborhoods or Both? Race and Ethnic Segregation and Educational Attainment." *Social Forces*, vol. 87, no. 4 (2009): 1913-1941.

Harris, Douglas N. "Lost Learning, Forgotten Promises: A National Analysis of School Racial Segregation, Student Achievement, and 'Controlled Choice' Plans." *Center for American Progress.* Washington, D.C; 2006.

Logan, John R., Elisabeta Minca, and Sinem Adar. "The Geography of Inequality: Why Separate Means Unequal in American Public Schools." *Sociology of Education*, vol. 85, no. 3 (2012): 287-301.

McCall, Martha S., Carl Hauser, John Cronin, G. Gage Kingsbury, and Ronald Houser. "Achievement Gaps: An Examination of Differences in Student Achievement and Growth." Northwest Evaluation Association. Portland, OR; 2006.

Mickelson, Roslyn Arlin, Martha Cecilia Bottia, Richard Lambert. "Effects of School Racial Composition on K–12 Mathematics Outcomes: A Metaregression Analysis." *Review of Educational Research*, vol. 83, no. 1 (2013): 121-158.

Owens, Ann. "Neighborhoods and Schools as Competing and Reinforcing Contexts for Educational Attainment." *Sociology of Education*, vol. 83, no. 4 (2010): 287-311.

Palardy, Gregory J. "High School Socioeconomic Segregation and Student Attainment." American Educational Research Journal, vol. 50, no. 4 (2013): 714-754.

Palardy, Gregory J. "Differential School Effects Among Low, Middle, and High Social Class Composition Schools: A Multiple Group, Multilevel Latent Growth Curve Analysis." *School Effectiveness and School Improvement: An International Journal of Research, Policy and Practice*, vol. 19, no. 1 (2008): 21-49.

Riegle-Crumb, Catherine and Eric Grodsky. "Racial-Ethnic Differences at the Intersection of Math Course-Taking and Achievement." *Sociology of Education*, vol. 83, no. 3 (2010): 248-270.

Rumberger, Russell W., "Parsing the Data on Student Achievement in High-Poverty Schools." *North Carolina Law Review*, vol. 85 (2007): 1293-1314.

Rumberger, Russell W. and Gregory J. Palardy. "Does Segregation Still Matter? The Impact of Student Composition on Academic Achievement in High School." *Teachers College Record*, vol. 107, no. 9 (2005): 1999-2045.

Ryabov, Igor. "Adolescent Academic Outcomes in School Context: Network Effects Reexamined." *Journal of Adolescence*, vol. 34 (2011): 915-927.

Ryabov, Igor and Jennifer Van Hook. "School Segregation and Academic Achievement Among Hispanic Children." *Social Science Research*, vol. 36 (2007): 767-788.

van Ewijk, Reyn and Peter Sleegers. "Peer Ethnicity and Achievement: A Meta-Analysis Into the Compositional Effect." *Tier Working Paper Series* (2010).

Appendix IV: Comments from the Department of Education

March 1, 2016

Ms. Jacqueline Nowicki
Director, Education, Workforce, and Income Security Issues
U.S. Government Accountability Office
441 G Street, NW
Washington, DC 20548

Dear Ms. Nowicki:

Thank you for providing the U.S. Department of Education (Education) the opportunity to review and comment on the U.S. Government Accountability Office (GAO) draft report entitled "K-12 Education: Better Use of Information Could Help Agencies Identify Disparities and Address Racial Discrimination" (GAO-16-345). The study examines (1) how the percentage of schools with high percentages of poor and Black or Hispanic students has changed over time and the characteristics of these schools, (2) why and how selected school districts have implemented actions to increase student diversity, and (3) to what extent the Departments of Education and Justice have taken actions to identify and address issues related to racial discrimination in schools.

GAO makes one recommendation for Education in the report, which is for the Office for Civil Rights (OCR) to "analyze its Civil Rights Data Collection by groupings and types of schools to further explore and understand issues and patterns of disparities. For example, Education could use this more detailed information to help identify issues and patterns among school types and groups in conjunction with its analyses of student groups." Thank you for the thoughtful recommendation. OCR already does analyze our Civil Rights Data Collection (CRDC) this way, both internally and for external consumption, and, in light of your recommendation, we will consider whether additional analysis could augment OCR's core civil rights enforcement mission.

The CRDC is a biannual data collection from school districts that collects a variety of information including student enrollment and educational programs and services, disaggregated by race/ethnicity, sex, limited English proficiency, and disability. The CRDC is a long-standing and important aspect of OCR's overall strategy for administering and enforcing the civil rights statutes for which it is responsible. As explained by Education officials to GAO during this study, CRDC data analysis is an important piece of information used in OCR investigations including in the process for identifying appropriate proactive compliance reviews. In those internal, data-driven decision processes, OCR often uses the types of analyses recommended by GAO in this report when appropriate. However, it is imperative to note that racial disparities are only one potential element for an investigation into whether discrimination is occurring in a school or school district.

OCR publishes data analyses based on data from the CRDC periodically. Those data analyses have included some of the kinds of analysis suggested in GAO's recommendation. Specifically, in OCR's data snapshots on College and Career Readiness and on Teacher Equity, analyses were conducted comparing schools attended by relatively high and low populations of students of color. OCR is currently finalizing the 2013-14 CRDC collection, which we hope will be ready for public release in the spring of 2016. Concurrent with publishing privacy-protected data on the ocrdata.cd.gov website, OCR plans to publish additional data analyses similar to those from the 2011-12 collection. OCR is already planning some of the analysis suggested in GAO's recommendation and will consider whether additional analysis would be helpful.

Information collected by the CRDC is also used by other Education offices as well as policymakers and researchers outside of Education. The publicly available data also allows secondary users to merge the CRDC with other data sets. OCR uses the National Center for Education Statistics (NCES) Identification (ID) to facilitate the cross-tabulation of data from other collections with CRDC data. For example, OCR makes free and reduced price lunch eligibility data available on our data reporting website and in data files as a courtesy with citation to NCES, which actually collects those data. The disaggregations of the data conducted by GAO are the type of specialized analyses that OCR encourages secondary users to explore.

Education appreciates that GAO's report draws attention to the robust activities the Department takes to address educational equity and the continuing efforts to desegregate schools across the nation. Promoting educational equity is the core of the mission of Education. To that end, Acting Secretary John King has continued and enhanced our efforts to encourage diverse schools through discretionary grant programs. Additionally, OCR maintains a continued focus on robust enforcement of Federal civil rights laws. We are committed to using every tool at our disposal to ensure that all students have access to an excellent education.

Thank you for your work on these important issues and for your consideration of our comments. Education is also providing technical comments and suggestions on the draft report. If you have additional questions or need additional information, we remain available to assist you. We look forward to receiving the final report.

Sincerely,

Catherine E. Lhamon
Assistant Secretary for Civil Rights

Appendix V: Comments from the Department of Justice

U.S. Department of Justice

Civil Rights Division

Deputy Assistant Attorney General

Washington, D.C. 20530

Jacqueline M. Nowicki   **MAR 0 8 2016**
Director
Education, Workforce, and Income Security Issues
U.S. Government Accountability Office
Washington, D.C. 20548

Dear Ms. Nowicki:

Thank you for the opportunity to review the final draft of the Government Accountability Office (GAO) report entitled "K-12 EDUCATION: Better Use of Information Could Help Agencies Identify Disparities and Address Racial Discrimination" (GAO-16-345). The draft report was reviewed by the Department of Justice's component that participated in the audit interviews. This letter constitutes the Department's formal comments. I request that the GAO include this letter as an attachment to the final version of the report.

Recommendations for Executive Action

We recommend that the Attorney General of the United States direct the Department of Justice's Civil Rights Division to systematically track key summary information across its portfolio of open desegregation cases and use this data to inform its monitoring of these cases. Such information could include, for example, dates significant actions were taken or reports received.

Comments Regarding Recommendation

While the Department of Justice agrees that tracking information concerning its litigation docket is important and useful, the Civil Rights Division notes that this recommendation may be premised on an erroneous understanding of the Division's role, as counsel for the United States, in the open desegregation cases to which the United States is a party. Additionally, the report reflects a lack of understanding about the Division's document management procedures. The Department carefully monitors each open desegregation case to which the United States is a party on a case-by-case basis, recognizing that each case is unique. The Department believes its procedures for tracking case-related data is adequate. Nevertheless, consistent with GAO's recommendation, the Division is currently developing an electronic document management system that may allow more case-related information to be stored in an electronic format.

However, the Division has a number of concerns regarding the report. The Division is concerned to the extent the report could be read to suggest that racial disparities within a public school district constitute *per se* evidence of racial discrimination. The Supreme Court has held that "one-race, or virtually one-race, schools within a district [that is operating under court supervision] is not, in and of itself, the mark of a system that still practices segregation by law."[1] While racial disparities in a school system which has not been declared unitary warrant close scrutiny, the critical question in every desegregation case is whether the school district has eliminated the vestiges of its prior *de jure* segregation to the extent practicable. This is a fact-specific inquiry that often requires the parties to engage in extensive discovery and develop a voluminous evidentiary record. Moreover, every school district and its related desegregation case is unique and decided on its individual merits, and therefore, must be considered on a case-by-case basis. For this reason, unlike the Department of Education, the Department does not maintain the type of aggregated school data the GAO staff requested during its audit.

The Division is concerned by the report's apparent criticism of the Division's actions in one case involving irregularities in test scores, which presents very complex legal and factual issues. The Division must consider and assess multiple factors before filing a pleading with the court or seeking specific action by a school district when racial disparities in a school system's operations are identified. Such actions involve, *inter alia*, decisions related to litigation strategy and the allocation of limited Department resources and personnel. Moreover, the existence of racial disparities in test scores alone is insufficient to trigger a remedy under the Division's legal authority, particularly when such disparities also exist in school districts that have not operated a *de jure* segregated system. The Division also is concerned with the report's emphasis on one phrase (..."if Justice had 'been keeping an eye' on relevant information...") from a footnote in a 107-page court opinion, which characterizes the case as having a long period of dormancy based solely on the absence of entries on the court's docket sheet. In this case and in many others, the Division often engages in case-related activities, such as site visits, requests for information, meetings and conferences, correspondence and settlement negotiations, which are not recorded on the courts' docket sheets.

The Division is concerned that the report could be read to suggest that some cases have remained "dormant" or "languished" for long periods as a result of the Department's data tracking system, without sufficient appreciation for the responsibilities of school districts and courts in advancing and resolving the cases. Each school district that operates under a desegregation order has a continuing affirmative duty to desegregate its schools, and school districts have the burden of proving to the courts that they are entitled to a declaration of unitary status and dismissal of the case. The courts alone have the authority to issue orders and compel districts to comply with their extant orders.[2] The United States is a litigating party to these cases; the Department does not "oversee" them. Indeed, the Division sometimes must seek court approval to obtain relevant information concerning school district activities because some court orders do not require the school district to provide information to the United States.

The report also fails to appreciate the extensive amount of data the Division maintains concerning its school desegregation cases and the limited purpose for which the data is collected.

---

[1] *Swann v. Charlotte-Mecklenburg Board of Education*, 402 U.S. 1, 26 (1970).

[2] The Division does not mean to diminish the role of the United States or the importance of any other plaintiff in a civil action, but the Supreme Court has clarified the allocation of responsibilities in desegregation cases. See *Swann*, 402 U.S. at 15-16.

2

Consistent with its responsibilities and authorities, Division employees track and preserve information received from school districts. All case-related correspondence and pleadings, for example, are recorded and retained by Division staff. The data the Division collects concerning its desegregation cases, however, are used predominately for the purposes of litigating each individual case. Thus, the Department does not track such data across cases.

Finally, the Division is concerned that various terms and recommendations in the report are not defined and/or clarified. The report, for example, states that "Justice does not systematically track key data to inform actions on open desegregation cases," but does not explain what it means by "systematically" and "key" data. The report also references "important summary information" without elaboration, and it does not explain what constitutes "significant actions" or the "last action" in the context of these complex cases. As noted above, the Division does have a process and system for tracking case-related correspondence and litigation documents. It is unclear what GAO, in the context of a desegregation case, might consider "key" or "important" information or a "significant action." The Division also has several mechanisms for determining what has transpired in any given case, depending on the type of investigation.[3] Attorneys, for example, may review the case correspondence files and court docket entries to identify the correspondence, reports pleadings, and orders issued in the case.

The Division's comments seek to clarify the extent to which the Civil Rights Division tracks case-related information in the context of each of its individual desegregation cases, and the nature of the case-by-case analysis that is required to successfully litigate these cases. The Department of Justice shares the GAO's goal of ensuring that the Division accurately and adequately tracks case-related information. Thank you for your staff's efforts to produce the report and the opportunity to work with them on these important issues.

Sincerely,

Eve L. Hill
Deputy Assistant Attorney General

---

[3] It should be noted that the Division's website, which is referenced in footnote 62 of the report, provides the public with examples of the types of cases the Division litigates and the matters it has resolved. The website is not intended to identify all of the complaints the Division investigates or every case or matter on the Division's docket.

3

www.ingramcontent.com/pod-product-compliance
Lightning Source LLC
Chambersburg PA
CBHW052002280526
45793CB00005B/823